The Symbolic Weapons of Ritual Magic

Second Edition

A Practical guide to Making & Consecrating Ceremonial Regalia

A. C. Highfield

The Pyramidion Press

Copyright © 1983-2016 A. C. Highfield

First published 1983

This edition 2016

This revised edition features minor corrections with some new additions and has been edited to improve clarity compared to the original edition published by the Aquarian Press in 1983.

All rights reserved. No part of this publication may be reproduced, distributed, or transmitted in any form or by any means, including photocopying, recording, or other electronic or mechanical methods, without the prior written permission of the publisher, except in the case of brief quotations embodied in critical reviews and certain other noncommercial uses permitted by copyright law.

ISBN: 1540575292
ISBN-13: 978-1540575296

This edition published by The Pyramidion Press
www.pyramidionpress.com

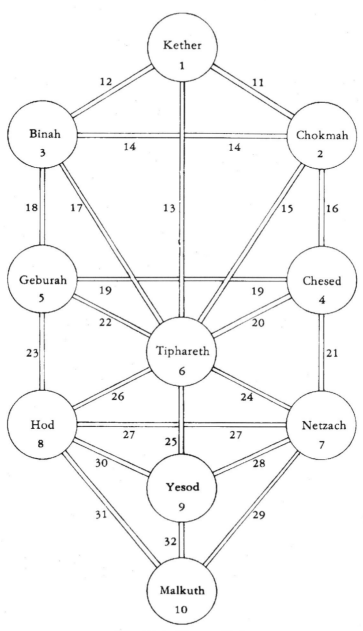

The Holy Tree of Life

BY THE SAME AUTHOR

The Book of Celestial Images
Meditation, Magic & The Tree of Life
Kabbalistic Magick in a Nutshell (*in press*)
Working with Inner Plane Teachers and Spirit Guides (*in preparation*)

A. C. Highfield has been a student of the Western mystery tradition for over 40 years. His previous works continue to be on the recommended reading lists of many esoteric schools, and are widely regarded as standard reference texts in their field. A lifelong vegetarian, he is also deeply committed to the cause of animal welfare, the promotion of tolerance and respect for all expressions of the True Self and the protection of our fragile environment. When not 'on his contacts' he is a scientist and a musician.

TABLE OF CONTENTS

1	Introduction	1
2	The Chalice on the Tree	4
3	The Rod on the Tree	25
4	The Sword on the Tree	45
5	The Pantacle on the Tree	67
6	The Minor Weapons on the Tree	84
7	Making the Weapons	91
8	Ritual Consecration of the Magical Weapons	115
	Appendix 1: The Pentagram and Hexagram Banishing Rituals	151
	Appendix II: Preparation of the Holy Water	164
	Appendix III: Pronunciation of Enochian	166
	Appendix IV: The Hebrew names used upon the weapons	168
	Table 1: The Sephiroth	170
	Table 2: The Colour Scales	171
	Table 3: Ritual Correspondences	172
	Bibliography	173
	Index	175

1 INTRODUCTION

The traditional 'armoury' of the magician, the sword, disc, cup and wand, together with the other paraphernalia of ceremonial magic is not at all as it may appear to the outsider. This is intentional, for to the initiate who understands their symbolism and function these ceremonial artefacts are powerful psychological 'triggers' capable of bringing about the profound awareness and concentration that typifies the transcendental state.

The function of these items may be likened to that of a computer keyboard. If the magician is correctly programmed, then applying the stimuli of the symbolic weapons will bring about accurate and predictable responses at all levels of consciousness. If the magician is not correctly 'programmed', then the application of the ceremonial weapons of magic will have at best no effect whatsoever and, at worst, potent but entirely unpredictable results. The mind is a delicate mechanism, and such 'Peeking' and 'Poking', to employ computer language terminology, within its circuits should only be attempted with full knowledge of the likely effects.

This book is an attempt to demonstrate the precision and logic of that seemingly most illogical art we call Qabalistic magic. The ancient symbols of cup, wand, disc and sword are revealed as the keys for gaining access to every level of individual consciousness, with a precision far in advance of most 'modern' schools of psychology.

Magic has been called 'the yoga of the West', an accurate summation. With the aid of the magic of the Western Mystery Tradition it is perfectly possible to climb every spiritual staircase. This is the aim and object of all real magic, which is not at all the 'easy way to get all you want' system of popular belief, but is instead a direct and demanding science of 'cleaving to God'. Magic always has been, and still is, an important spiritual undercurrent in the West, and if this book sheds a little light on its inner teachings and prompts others to take up the path, then I am well satisfied.

The preceding comments are aimed at the beginner, but I hope too that the more advanced student may benefit from the ideas express in this book. Wherever possible, I have attempted to explain fully my reasons for selecting a particular attribution and I hope that those who disagree on specific points will understand that it is not my intention to imply that their method is in any way incorrect or inferior to my own. I recognise that magic is very much an individual art, and that there are as many 'right' ways of doing things as there are individual magicians.

For the sake of brevity, and for no other reason, in this book and those that follow in this series, the masculine form of address is normally used in reference to the student, but it should be understood at all times that this implies 'herself' and 'she' as much as 'himself' and 'him'. Further, it is recognised that the outer form does not invariably coincide with inner realities, and that for the magician, inner realities may transcend the outer. Be true to who you are. Magic, true magic, rewards and respects truth, and there is no greater truth than unifying all aspect of the self and directing them to reflect and honour the 'True Will'.

Introduction

After much consideration I decided to include full length consecration rituals within the framework of this book. I did so in the full knowledge that some may question the wisdom of this action. However, I felt that the potential benefits to the serious lone student, probably isolated from any source of workable ritual material, greatly outweighed the possible disadvantages in revealing such material to the proverbial 'dabbler' - who would be unlikely to obtain any results even if the rituals were attempted.

This new edition of *"The Symbolic Weapons of Ritual Magic"* includes some minor corrections that 'slipped through the net' in the original Aquarian Press edition published in 1983. It is accompanied, too, by re-publication of its sister volume *"The Book of Celestial Images"* (1984), also in a revised edition, and *"Meditation, Magic and the Tree of Life"* which, after a 30-plus year delay, is now appearing for the very first time.

All that remains is for the student, of whatever level, to take up this book in the spirit in which it was written and to give thought to the unknown geniuses of ages past who devised the roots, which grew into a Tree, of which the Western Mystery Tradition is but one branch.

2 THE CHALICE ON THE TREE

The chalice is one of the few symbolic or so called 'elemental' tools that students of magic seem to agree about. Nearly all attribute it to water; it is usually considered feminine and passive in nature, and it is almost always taken as symbolising lunar forces and the forces of Yesod in particular.

The chalice, formed of a suitable leaf, was almost certainly one of the first 'tools' used by early man. Then, as now, it was at its most mundane level a container of liquids. It is at this level that we all meet it daily. It also exists on other, far deeper levels as we shall see, but for now let us examine its material expression in our everyday lives.

Although few give it any thought as they sip tepid coffee from a polystyrene cup at a railway station or airport terminal, they are in fact partaking of a ritual which, if expanded and meditated upon, is capable of opening up a whole panorama of human experience. At a deeper level this same ritual is enacted daily within many churches, where the chalice serves as a vessel containing the Holy Blood in the form of the communion wine. Somewhat lower down the spiritual ladder a very similar rite takes place each evening in your local club, pub or bar, where the contents of numerous chalices are 'consecrated' by blessing with a toast before being ritually consumed. It is true that such acts are usually carried out without any understanding of their origins, but if you doubt that they have significance, refuse to take a drink with someone who offers you one! Invariably you will be pressured into changing your mind. The person feels hurt or rejected, and this reflects the very deep levels to which seemingly simple and unimportant acts penetrate.

The magician also experiences these effects, but unlike his or her lay companion the magician realises why they are caused, and how to use them in his search for a greater truth.

We can confidently state that all the traditional tools or 'weapons' of the magician's art, the wand, chalice, sword and pantacle, are each capable of reaching very deep levels within the mind of the operator and of causing subtle changes within the microcosm that reflect into the macrocosm. *It is this ability to evoke responses within the subconscious mind of the operator that makes the tools 'magical'*. If they failed in this, then they would be useless as aids in exploring and influencing the strange realms behind the veils of everyday matter.

The best guide to these realms is without doubt the Qabalistic Tree of Life, and it is this which we shall use as we begin our exploration of the forces that we evoke within ourselves as we take up the tools of the art. For unless we understand these forces, how they interact, and the symbolism that is used to contact them, we shall surely fail in our attempt to reach them through the agency of cup, rod, sword and disc. The cup or chalice exists on many levels from the most mundane to the most esoteric and sublime, but at each level it is a potent tool that reacts in a predetermined fashion. In this it is like a computer. Insert the correct program, push the right buttons, and obtain the correct answers! The magician being the computer in this case, the tree the program, and the tools the buttons. The language used is not Basic or 'C', but symbolism.

Why must we speak in symbols? The answer is simple. The forms we hope to converse with are so vast, formless and abstract that without symbolic language we should not only fail to understand them we should fail even to perceive them.

We must resign ourselves then to much symbolism in the following pages, but instead of looking upon this as an esoteric waste of time, we should look upon it as the programming that will eventually enable us to expand our consciousness to regions where we may indeed walk one day with angels. In this light it is worth the effort it takes to learn their language.

In the Qabalistic Tree system all things originate in Kether, the sephirah at the very top of the glyph, and by various paths eventually find material expression in the lowest sephirah Malkuth, the sphere of mundane existence.

In this case we are attempting to trace our tools back to their origins and so must climb the tree from Malkuth to Kether even as man must do if he is to regain his rightful place in the cosmic scheme of things. We must not forget, however, that we are working 'upside down' as it were, and that the forces we meet flow from above, never from below. We shall now look at each sephirah (sphere) of the tree in turn as the water chalice appears at each level.

Malkuth

This is where the cup is a container of liquid, a barrier preventing spillage and a limiting factor to the expansion of the contents; where it receives whatever we place within it, only to give it up when directed by an external agency, deliberate or accidental.

The cup is never empty, even though it may appear so at first sight, for even if it is emptied of water, air at once takes its place, and even if it is placed in a total vacuum the cup is full of magnetic and atomic radiations, or of light or darkness. A cup is never truly empty.

This cup may bring us salvation in the form of water if we are dying of thirst in the desert or it may administer deadly poison in the form of cyanide or hemlock. That which sustains us may also carry the seeds of our eventual destruction.

The usual contents of the cup, however, are ordinary water and water is the supreme material agency of fertility and generation, for it contains and dissolves all the essential chemicals and nutrients needed to create and sustain life and transmits them to where they are required. It not only contains solids, but also gasses and to a lesser extent latent heat energy. Hence, it is a synthesis of the four alchemical elements of Earth, Air, Fire and Water on a material level.

A superb example of this in practice is blood, and understanding this it is easy to see why it has become so venerated and imbued with both magical and religious significance. Water is of course, the supreme medium of generation in an historical sense, for out of the nutrient rich primeval oceans, all life on this planet evolved. Water is not only a medium of creation; it is also a medium of dissolution and purification. It washes away the mud and dirt, both physical and spiritual, that they may be removed from our bodies and souls. In this guise it is frequently encountered as 'Holy Water' and in a similar manner it serves the ritualist as he "sprinkles with the lustral waters of the loud resounding sea", thereby dissolving any impurities and utilising the transmuting properties of water to return these undesired elements to the earth.

We are all familiar with the properties of physical water, cold, wet and fluid. Elemental or 'inner' water is similar, but of course we are now speaking of principals not physical actualities. Water flows, so do our emotions. Water can be prevented from flowing by damming it, but if the pressure reaches a critical level the dam will burst, with disastrous consequences. The same is true of 'pent up' emotions. Inner elements, then, are not lakes of water, mountains of rock, volcanoes of fire or force ten gales but vital principles expressing a similar nature to their physical counterparts. In fact the ritualist often visualises the inner elements in a physical form, but only so that he can concentrate upon what are in actuality abstract forces. To visualise them as described above aids the concentration and brings them within reach of human perception, but at no time does the magician forget that the images he sees are anything but man-made forms for the abstract principles that lie behind them to inhabit.

On these inner levels elemental water is a carrier of consciousness and the term 'Sea of Consciousness' is an ideal metaphor in this context. This inner water is not cold or threatening in any way, but is instead sustaining, friendly and protective. In excess it may be unstabilising, but taken in moderation it can only be of benefit to us. This applies to all elemental forces, as it does to everything else. This inner elemental water, then, may be regarded with the other elements of Air, Fire, and Earth as one of the four principal forces behind manifestation of every type.

These forces exist in their pure state only in very rare circumstances, and in general a particular manifestation is derived from a mixture of these elements. When the elements do manifest in their pure or unmixed state these pure units of specialised energy are termed 'Elemental Spirits' and in the case of water these are known as undines. These spirits or energy units have no intelligence in the normal sense and know of nothing outside their own environment. In this they could be termed 'mindless spirits' but, as we shall see, if we contact them on inner levels they are by no means ignorant of their own realms, where they function under the direction of more versatile and powerful units of specialised energy termed angels.

The Elementals are beings, in a sense, who are undergoing evolution; what they lack is the ability to understand or function outside of their own element; above all they lack the gift of spirit. This they frequently hope to earn by serving mankind, who has it within his power to help them to attain this prize. Without it they are doomed to extinction. The angels with direct responsibility for the elementals are the Kerubim, a higher version of the elements themselves, being comprised of an ox, eagle, lion and man. These may be recognised as the fixed zodiacal signs of Taurus, Scorpio, Leo and Aquarius (this description of the physical form of an angel may come as a surprise if you are used to the Christianised versions usually depicted. Nonetheless it is entirely accurate.) We can usefully make an analogy with a large factory to understand the 'chain of command' that governs the responsibilities of the various otherworld potencies we term elementals, angels, archangels and god-aspects. Elementals function in the world of Assiah, where they may be likened to power-operated tools of specialist application. Angels, who function in the world of Yetzirah, are the production line workers who apply the power tools to the best effect. They are skilled craftsmen, but only in their own speciality. Their departmental managers are termed archangels and their region is known to Qabalists as Briah. The president of the corporation has ultimate control over everything, but of course does not concern himself directly with control over the individual departments, and still less with the welding torch or spray gun wielded by the production workers. His boardroom is located in the god-aspect world of Atziluth. To meet the archangel of water we must leave Malkuth and the world of the elemental spirits and enter the next sphere on the tree.

Yesod

The mighty archangel of water and the lunar sephirah Yesod is Gabriel, one of the better known, in name at least, of the four elemental archangels. We shall meet his counterparts for air, fire and earth in due course. Gabriel is most famed as the Holy Angel of the annunciation, thus fulfilling one of his traditional duties as divine messenger. But this conceals an important truth, for the real function of Gabriel is not merely to announce fertility, but to initiate it. The clue may be found in the symbolism of the horn with which he is usually depicted. This has been misinterpreted by Christian theologians as a 'trumpet of awakening', and to a certain extent it does function on these lines, but it does not by some miraculous means cause the physical resurrection of corpses; rather, it works its miracle in accordance with natural laws, as indeed do all genuine manifestations of divine will.

The horn is a symbol of immense potency, in a literal sense, for it is the supreme symbol of sexual fertility. Externally, it is reminiscent of the phallus, and internally the vagina. Small wonder that it is thus venerated the world over, although in the West we often fail to recognise it even when we confront it at close quarters.

Our less 'civilised' ancestors were not so blind! J. G. Frazer's monumental work *"The Golden Bough"*, a veritable encyclopedia of folk belief and customs, and Robert Graves's equally important work *"The White Goddess"* both give examples of the cornucopia and cauldron of plenty aspects of the horn. It is in these forms that the horn symbol still survives in something like its original form in the folk customs and practices of rural communities in the more isolated parts of the world.

This same regenerative concept may be found in the ark symbols of many religious systems, from the Egyptian to the Celtic Arthurian myths as well as the famed Noah's ark of the bible. In the latter instance the ark is a container of the genetic material of entire species, and in the first two examples the ark is a container of the spiritual essence of a divine king; the boat sailing on the sea of darkness carrying the spirit into the regeneration of light.

An ark, a horn, a cup and a cauldron are all symbols allocated to Yesod and to the concept of birth and rebirth. Nowhere does the term 'drink of the cup of life' apply better than in Yesod under the direction of Gabriel.

A crystal clear reiteration of this may be found in the Hebrew God-name of Sephirah Yesod, *Shadai El Chai*, which translated into English means 'powerful overlord of life'. The mundane chakra, or planetary aspect of Yesod is the moon, and this too is of great significance if we are to fully comprehend the elemental water and sexual regeneration aspects dealt with so far.

The famed mystical 'Emerald Tablet' posed a riddle that has direct relevance here. It asked that we should discover what is meant by *"The sun its father, the moon its mother, the wind hath carried it to the womb thereof, it descendeth from Heaven unto Earth"*. The answer, of course, is life itself.

In ritual usage, the moon-water-womb concept is symbolised by the chalice, a more sophisticated form of horn, and the sun-fire-phallus concept by the fire weapons, rod or sword according to your chosen attribution system. Throughout occult and mythological literature this theme of the male, positive force of the sun, and the female, receptive force of the moon is encountered. This is ritually enacted in the Wicca rites of union, sometimes referred to as 'The Great Rite' where the fire weapon, usually the sacred athame, the witch's knife, is lowered into the water chalice with the words *"Lance to grail, spear to cauldron, fire to water, athame to cup"*, the intent being that *"conjoined they bring blessedness to life"*. The lunar link of the cup and sephirah Yesod is also found in the mirror images associated with them, in particular, the reflected image of the moon in the sacred chalice, cauldron or well. The fairy tale 'Mirror, mirror, on the wall' material is derived from these sources, half-forgotten race memories of ancient 'Drawing Down the Moon' rites, when the image of the moon was 'captured' in a sacred cup or cauldron and then questioned about future events and fortunes, good and bad. Major decisions concerning whole tribes and kingdoms were frequently based upon such magically derived information, and it was obviously considered entirely reliable or it would not have persisted as long as it did. The very same methods used by the Romans and Egyptians were still in use, in isolated parts of Britain, up to the early part of this century. A pale reflection still persists in the seaside fortune teller's crystal ball, crystal being a major magical correspondence of both the moon and sephirah Yesod.

The moon has three important goddesses assigned to her: Diana, mistress of magic and hunting; Hecate, also queen of enchantments, and the Celtic Ana. It should be noted that moon goddesses fall into three categories, Virgin, Mother and Hag, and that these are linked to the lunar phases. It is most important to bear this in mind, for this cycle is vital to our understanding of both the ancient mythologies and our magical cup. To sum up, we can say that the chalice in Yesod is symbolic of the lunar currents, the feminine sexual principal on a higher level than expressed in Malkuth and of 'second sight', or etheric vision as it is termed by occultists. To gain further insights into the symbolism of our chalice we must leave the moon sephirah Yesod and its reflective, magical images and enter the sphere of another goddess, Venus, and the sephirah Netzach.

Netzach

Sephirah Netzach is essentially concerned with victory and achievement, as its name states in straightforward terms, the victory being the victory of divine love, against all odds, and the achievement being the achievement of a parent in transmitting their genetic lineage via the successful rearing of children. Netzach is survival in a 'do or die' sense. The passion of a mother, prepared to lay down her life if need be that her offspring may survive.

But Netzach goes much further than this, for rather than remain concerned with individuals Netzach functions on a far wider basis. We shall examine this aspect in a few moments, but first let us look at the cup as it appears in Netzach.

The cup of Yesod is transformed in Netzach by the influx of Geburic fire via the 24th part of the tree into an initiatory sex drive version of tremendous potency. If the cup of Yesod is the cup of fertility, then the cup of Netzach is the cup of passion, which initiates that fertility. Without sexual attraction there would be very little sex and with little or no sex there would be very little fertility. Yesod is the sphere of sexual union, but it is Netzach that places the desire for sex there in the first instance. The sexual aspect of Netzach is most important, and it has long been at the roots of many manifestations of 'religious sex' as practised in the temples of ancient Greece and Rome, for instance, or more recently by certain occult groups. Whilst in many cases these practices were merely indulgences, in the genuine mystery temples they were used with reverence and great effect, for they were based upon sound principals.

The 'base element' of sephirah Netzach is water; this is then energised by the reflected fire from Geburah in a union of perfect opposites. The nearest humans can get to this perfect union is the sexual union of male and female, fire and water, lance to grail. Understanding this, much of the 'sex magic' practised by the late

Aleister Crowley makes a good deal more sense. The essence of Crowley's magic was the creation of a vital 'elixir' from the mingled sexual fluids of the self-appointed 'Beast 666' and his assistant, the 'Scarlet Woman'. Now while these practices may revolt the sensitive and draw forth gasps of horror from the inhibited, they doubtless have a basis that is symbolically, if not actually, accurate.

Much of the significance of these practices is clear from the titles assumed by the participants, and also from the other terminology used by Crowley in his extensive diaries. Since this has a direct relevance to one aspect of sephirah Netzach and our magical cup we shall examine these techniques in some detail.

Crowley assumed the title 'Beast 666' because it symbolised the Solar Logos and is essentially composed of a union of fire and light. It is totally solar-phallic in nature. The 'Scarlet Woman', on the other hand, is composed (elementally speaking) of a combination of water, enthused with fire; this is apparent not only from her title (which reflects Fire and Red = Mars-Geburah and Woman = Lunar-Yesod) but in her chief asset, 'the Cup of Babalon', which is none other than her *kteis*. The cup, as we have seen, is always feminine, whether it be in Yesod or Netzach. The main clue, however, as to the reasoning behind these operations can be found in the names allocated to the sexual fluids themselves. The male sexual fluid was entitled the 'Blood of the Red Lion' and the female fluid 'The Gluten of the White Eagle'. This is revealing, for the Red Lion is the symbol of the fire Kerub and the white eagle is the water Kerub, Leo and Scorpio in conjunction, their respective weapons being the sword-lance and the cup-grail. Leo would find a general attribution in Geburah and Scorpio in Yesod; but conjoined they are placed in Netzach. These sexual workings were frequently known as 'Observances of the Mass of the Holy Ghost' and this would fit in perfectly with a lower manifestation of divinity in Yesod, the etheric region attributed to the Holy Ghost.

It should be added, that Crowley concocted a secret 11th degree of initiation concerned with homosexual magic (heterosexual magic being 9th degree) and attributed this to Hod, the balanced opposite of Netzach at the base of the negative black pillar of the Tree. This will be looked at in some detail when dealing with the wand, and sephirah Hod in particular.

Some students of the Qabalah might dispute the attribution of the cup to Netzach, insisting that the proper symbol is the lamp. The truth is that both symbols are equally at home, the fruits of the Tree being many faceted; which particular face you happen to see depends to a great extent upon which angle you approach them from. While the lamp is an excellent symbol of the illumination and initiation aspects of Netzach, the cup is a far superior symbol of the woman seeking man sexual aspect. We should not make the grave mistake of over simplification where the Tree is concerned and attempt to apply absolute rules and regulations to it. This is always deficient, and leads only to petty disputes over minor attributions and correspondences. To say that Netzach consists only of elemental water (or fire) is missing out on at least half the picture. If we fail to take in all of the scenery, we can hardly complain later that we did not learn much on our travels.

A good way to visualise the 28th path from Netzach to Yesod is to imagine Gabriel holding out his cup in the silver light of Yesod, whilst above him Haniel, the archangel of Netzach, directs a beam of pure life force into it. Gabriel then administers this to the inhabitants of Malkuth in measured quantities. If we bypassed his wise rationing we should run the grave risk of becoming 'drunk on life' and burning ourselves out rather rapidly through over indulgence in sex, sensation, and pleasure seeking of various ecstatic varieties. This idea of life force and the transmission of genetic information in the form of a 'Blood Royal' is very closely related to Netzach, where it takes one of the most famous of all mystical forms - the Holy Grail.

The grail is essentially a container of blood, holy blood, within a cup. If we recognise that we ourselves are nothing more than cups, mere containers of blood, then we begin to get a clearer picture of what the grail actually is. It was once believed that certain individuals, mainly kings or other spiritual leaders, were actually descended from gods; it is obvious from this that their blood was held to be very precious and why the penalties for harming the royal personage were so severe, the penalties for 'tainting' the royal blood through unauthorised sexual activity with such individuals being only slightly less horrendous! The reasoning behind all this is faultless, given the absolute belief that the divine king and his immediate relations are incarnate gods. Since they represented the spiritual 'power base' of the tribe or kingdom, to taint their purity would be to attack and weaken the race as a whole - treason was never popular in any age. In early times it was also believed that the gift of 'second sight' or etheric clairvoyance was maintained and transmitted by a direct blood link with the priesthood or priestess-hood. That this belief was still current up to a couple of centuries ago is painfully apparent from the maniacal desire of the self-appointed 'witch finders' to massacre even distant relatives of alleged witches and sorcerers, up to and including cousins thrice removed. The same belief still prevails in isolated parts of Ireland and Scotland to this day, where the seventh son of a seventh son is accorded the benefit of 'the gift' in popular parlance.

To the working magician one of the major lessons of Netzach is concerned with its initiation and awakening aspects, for the fires of Mars-Geburah combined with the waters of Venus-Netzach are a potent means of releasing 'inner steam' and forcing open new pathways and inner contacts. This is symbolised by the lamp, mentioned above, which can be viewed as the 'Lucifer - Light Bringer' aspect of Venus as it rises over a bitter sea, both symbols we shall encounter again later. This Lucifer link also makes a certain amount of sense if we consider Lucifer in Christian terms as a supreme tempter of the flesh. Nowhere is more suited to this than Netzach.

To summarise: Netzach's Cup is essentially one of awakened sexual urges, of woman seeking man, of water reacting under heat and of the blood link of the Holy Grail. The awakening of Netzach refers to awakening of sexual polarity, inner contacts and these result ultimately in fertility in Yesod - genetic fertility and mental fertility. Success on these levels results in Victory and Achievement, the passwords to sephirah Netzach. We now leave Netzach and follow the path of the divine king as he meets his doom in Tiphareth, where we again encounter the grail.

Tiphareth

Sephirah Tiphareth is central to the design and function of the Tree; it is a place where opposing forces must be reconciled and where the true nature of the Great Work is expressed in practice. It is difficult to examine sephirah Tiphareth in the light of just one aspect, for it encompasses all aspects in equal proportion and importance. We shall encounter Tiphareth several times later, in particular when dealing with the fire weapons; but for now we must be content to take only a general look at it and limit ourselves temporarily to a brief examination as it pertains to the Divine King and the grail.

The scope covered by sephirah Tiphareth is truly vast, as might be expected of a sphere which encompasses all things in a vision of harmony. This is one of its dangers to the unwary seeker, for it is very easy indeed to obtain a false message based upon a partial sight of its extensive scenery. The only valid vision of Tiphareth is one which takes into account all its aspects, and this is no small task, physically or spiritually.

Tiphareth may be easier to understand in the light of the god-forms allocated to it. These include all 'mediator-redeemer' figures, including Christ, Osiris and indeed all similar solar logos deities. The mundane chakra of Tiphareth is the Sun, and this in itself is a clear indication of the nature of the sephirah, the burning light of illumination which chases away the darkness of night. The night in this case is a spiritual darkness dissolved by the application of divine light received by the god-king from Kether, and reflected by him into Malkuth.

It is almost always the fate of solar deities that they must be sacrificed in order to release their spiritual reservoir of 'redeemer power'. This may be seen not only in the sacrifice of Christ or Osiris, but out in the cornfields where the 'corn king' was ritually killed to liberate his spirit that it might return to the sun when the harvest was over. This sacrifice was usually accomplished by stabbing or by burning, both being representative of fire force liberating the energy contained within the incarnate god's own blood.

The god-name of sephirah Tiphareth is *Yhvh Aloah va Daath*, not an easy name to translate as it can be taken as symbolic of many new things. The usual meaning behind it is considered to be 'Lord God of Knowledge', in the sense of spiritual, not factual knowledge. The archangel of Tiphareth is undoubtedly Michael, not Raphael as is sometimes given, and it is Michael who mediates between severity and Geburah on his left hand and mercy and Chesed on his right - Geburah symbolising the sword-tip of his spear, and Chesed the shaft. This is an important image, for it sums up the mediation and reconciliation aspects of Tiphareth rather well. This spear symbol is also interesting in the light of Christ's death on the Calvary cross of sacrifice, where his side was pierced by a spear allowing water to run out, a grim reminder of the 'spear to cauldron, lance to grail' formula we encountered earlier. These aspects will be dealt with in more depth as we trace the symbolic development of the fire weapons, and the incarnation theme of the Divine King will be found also in our pantacle symbol. But for now we must leave Tiphareth and enter the martial sephirah of Geburah, where we find the source of the fire reflected into Netzach.

Geburah

This sephirah will be dealt with in considerable detail when examining the attributions of the fire weapons, but, for now, we need only take note of the chalice aspects of Geburah. That Geburah has a chalice aspect at all will surprise some students; but whilst Geburah may appear entirely masculine and positive, this is far from the whole truth. No sephirah is entirely one kind of force, and Geburah is no exception.

Geburah is placed on the black, negative receptive pillar under Binah for good reason. The reason being that Geburah is the feminine aspect of masculinity. Mars was essentially a warrior goddess, something along the lines of the Hindu Kali. Further confirmation of this link can be obtained when we realise that the ancient Semites had a goddess of war and love whom they knew as Anat. Where Netzach is the essence of masculinity expressed within femininity, Geburah is femininity expressed within masculinity. No male is one hundred percent male and no female is one hundred percent female; we are all bisexual to a certain degree, if only inwardly.

We find a link also in that both Binah and Geburah have a common image in the mother who devours her children. The function of Geburah, too, is feminine, in that it represents the negative polarity of creative power. The woman must first receive the seed before giving birth, and the power 'born' in Geburah is male fire. The 'son' of the warrior goddess is the male aspect of Geburah; she herself is of course female. This has caused a great deal of confusion in the past and many people seem to have forgotten that a female aspect of Geburah ever existed. It most certainly did, and has significance to our understanding of both the Tree and our water chalice, which symbolises this aspect. It should not be forgotten either that the colour associated with Geburah and Mars is blood red, and as we have seen this is frequently also associated with our chalice symbol as a container of blood. To really find the roots of our chalice we must leave Geburah, where it is a minor symbol, and progress to the supernal triad and sephirah Binah, where the origination of the chalice may be found in the great bitter sea, the primal waters of the Great Mother.

Binah

Sephirah Binah is the third of the great supernals, and according to Qabalistic doctrine has its own origination in Chokmah, directly opposite it on the male pillar. The magical image of Binah is the vision of a mature woman, and its titles Ama, the dark sterile mother, and Aima, the bright fertile mother, are most revealing when taken in conjunction with the vast amount of mythological data pertaining to the archetypal Great Mother.

Binah is the first sephirah of form; it receives as impregnating agency the pure force radiated by Chokmah and transmutes this into force contained by form. In this it is also the archetypal chalice. In essence it is the womb of the universe. The word 'Ama' is formed of the Hebrew letter *'Mem'*, which symbolises water, between two *Aleph's*, signifying the beginning of things. More specifically, *Aleph* means an ox, and this is familiar to us as the kerubic sign of Earth, the ultimate manifestation of material form. Aima is the same word with the addition of *Yod*, an active letter, initiating its fertility. Aima gives birth, and Ama extends her arms to receive her child on the return journey after life experience. It is Ama the disciplinarian whom we encountered in another aspect of Geburah, and Aima whom we encountered in Netzach as Aphrodite or Venus.

If we think back to the moon goddesses of Yesod, virgin, mother and hag, we can place the mother and hag aspects in Aima and Ama respectively, with the virgin as unactivated potential attributed to the point of equilibrium between Chokmah and Binah on the middle pillar, i.e., that which would become the mother before the mother sephirah Binah was formed. This is a difficult concept, but relates to a time continuum which existed after the formation of Chokmah, but prior to the formation of Binah. Any form attributed to Binah is bound to seem somewhat vague in certain respects, for Binah is beyond the range of normal human consciousness, and functions in entirely archetypal forms. This makes it rather difficult to grasp at times, for humans tend to over sentimentalise, or attempt to attribute human qualities to everything they meet. At supernal levels on the Tree such methods are apt to yield inaccurate and misleading results. An example of this is the reaction of some students upon learning that Ama, the dark mother, has as one of her symbols the mother who devours her own offspring. "Oh, how terrible!", they say, without actually thinking about this in cosmic, rather than human terms. In non-human terms this is merely the 'recycling' of redundant or defective material that it may later be reused to build new forms for life to inhabit.

In Binah we find many of the same symbols that we encountered in Yesod, for both Binah and Yesod have close ties with lunar-type forces. The mundane chakra assigned to Binah is Saturn, and this is highly significant not only in respect of the Kronos (time) link (of which more in a moment) but in the less obvious fact that Saturn has nine moons and that nine is also the sacred number of the Earth's moon in many mythologies. If this is a coincidence, then it is bordering on the miraculous, for the chances against it being so must be stacked rather high, and of course at the time these attributions were laid down telescopes were inventions of the far distant future. Did our ancestors have access to rather more sophisticated astronomical information than it is now customary to give them credit for? Other strange 'coincidences' along similar lines tend to suggest that they did.

This link with the number nine, the moon, and femininity is apparent in nearly all ancient religious systems. The number nine being the usual period of gestation in months of human beings, and the moon and lunar tides, of course, have always been closely associated with menstruation. Exactly how all this symbolism was worked out by so-called savages is a matter of speculation!

The angel order of Binah are the Aralim, which translates as 'Thrones'. The reason for this is clear enough if we recognise that a throne is merely a seat of power. Binah is the throne that receives the king power of Chokmah and gives it foundation in form. It applies the restriction and discipline required to mould abstract forces into archetypal forms. This, then, is the duty of the Aralim, who may be visualised as glittering chalices of differing designs 'stamping out' prototype archetypal forms, then returning to refill with pure god-force at the well of Chokmah force, ever bubbling, overflowing with abstractions were it not for the tireless effort of the Aralim in emptying it as quickly as it fills.

We must leave them to their task and meet the overlord, the archangel of Binah, Tzaphkiel. This mighty archangel is termed 'the watcher of God' and we shall see in our examination of the fire weapons that he has strong links with Satan, the bright one. The mythology here is complex, but we must not make the mistake of assuming that Tzaphkiel is in any way evil; such a concept in the context of the divine Tree is entirely misplaced; but his role as the eye of god has frequently been unwelcome by humans who would rather keep their dark deeds secret! A better illustration may be found in the 'Eye of Horus' symbol of the Egyptians, where the burning eye of the son of Isis and the slain Osiris was held to be ever watchful and ready to do battle with evil forces. The eye of Horus in its 'watcher' mode may be likened to Tzaphkiel, and in its destroyer-by-fire aspect it is remarkably similar to Khamael, the archangel of sephirah Geburah.

The god-name for Binah is *Ihvh Elohim*, which indicates 'God the Mother' as opposed to 'God the Father'. This 'mother' aspect was suppressed by fanatical anti-feminist Rabbis, and eventually Yahwe the Father triumphed, at least as far as popular religion was concerned. The feminine 'Eloh' still survived in the mystery traditions however. The spiritual experience assigned to Binah is the 'Vision of Sorrow' and nowhere is this better illustrated than by the various god-forms associated with this aspect of the sephirah.

The mother of sorrows appears in many guises, from the Greek Demeter sorrowing for her daughter Persephone, to the tragic Isis mourning for her lost Osiris and the very similar legends associated with Aphrodite and Adonis, or Cybele and Attis, this last pair being famed for the barbaric practices of their priests, who ritually castrated themselves with sickles. The sickle as we have discovered is the ritual 'correspondence' of Saturn. Another card drops neatly into place in our cosmic filing system. Christian Qabalists frequently draw upon the symbol of the mourning Mary at the foot of the cross of crucifixion, and indeed this is a legitimate image in this context. It should also be noted that the Virgin Mary is known by the alternative title of Stella Maris, 'Star of the Sea' - an excellent allusion to her 'other' side, a goddess of Aima, the bright fertile mother. Mythologically speaking, the bright star of the sea is Venus or Lucifer, and this in turn is related to the so-called 'Scarlet Woman'. There is much room for meditation upon these aspects of Christian symbolism, which conceal many inner mysteries.

At this stage we have returned to the same symbols with which we began: the cup as a restrictor-container, but on a much higher level than manifested in Malkuth, or reflected in Yesod. A veritable plethora of cups, chalices, cauldrons, arks, seas, wells, mirrors and lakes, etc. The list is almost endless. But all these things are linked by the forces they represent, and indeed evoke, within human consciousness. For millennia these symbols have been used by priests, priestesses and magicians to make that vital inner link which is the basis of all real magic. They are no less valid today than they were 6,000 years ago and longer. We have come a long way from our polystyrene cup in a railway station! In the process we have grasped something of the essence of the magical nature of a simple everyday object. We must now leave the water cup and set out on a second journey through the Tree of Life to discover the origins of another of our magical ritual weapons, the staff or rod.

3 THE ROD ON THE TREE

The general comments upon symbolism and the order of creation made with regard to the water chalice still apply in respect of the air wand, so it will not be necessary to repeat these observations in detail here. It should also be recognised that where a particular sephirah is under discussion we are dealing with only one aspect of it, and not attempting to give a total picture. This is not a general guide to the Qabalah, merely a guide to the Tree as it relates specifically to the symbolic regalia of the magician. A total picture will emerge, but only after prolonged study, and certainly not until each of the four weapons has been dealt with in full.

Upon embarking on our rod voyage, we hit a major obstacle even before casting off, for there is a large measure of utter confusion and total disagreement as to what it actually symbolises. Some claim that it is a solar and phallic fire symbol, others that it is a solar-phallic air symbol! As can be imagined, this causes quite a fluttering in the occult dovecote, much of which filters through into the correspondence pages of occult news sheets and magazines. It seems that many people take it as a personal insult if someone else begs to differ with their pet attributions. So, grasping the dragon firmly by the tail, we shall plunge headfirst in to the quagmire and state that in this work we attribute the rod to the air element; but it should be thoroughly understood that neither attribution is wrong as long as it works for you, and that equally good results can be obtained using both systems. You are entirely free to use whichever attribution suits you best, and if the fire system makes those vital inner 'connections' then you should certainly use it. If this is the case, simply substitute 'fire' for 'air', and trace your weapons using the combined information of both rod and sword sections. With this out of the way let us now look at our air wand or rod as it appears in Malkuth.

Malkuth

The rod in our system is symbolic of elemental air; it is also a tool in the mundane sense that it forms the basis of all measurement, and without the rod mankind would be in a rather sorry and primitive state. If you doubt this startling assertion, then try and imagine a world in which the rod was never invented, or discovered. There would be no wheels, for there would be no spokes or axles; no radio or television for antennae would be impossible; no spears, arrows, rulers, electricity, piped water, writing or a host of other vital things which make our world into a habitable place. Without mundane rods we would lack transport and communication in particular, and our magical rods are every bit as vital if we are attempting to transport on inner levels and communication with inner plane potencies.

As a pen, a rod writes and communicates intelligence, as an axle it helps to propel us along. Where would we be without rods? Immobile and ignorant, and the magician is just as immobile or ignorant of inner realities if deprived of his magical rod. For this reason the magician values his rod above all else, for it is a vital part of his being, the means by which he talks with his or her gods and the means by which one day he hopes to travel to join them.

Another aspect of the rod in Malkuth is the rod of punishment and reward, the rod of severity and mercy. If the rod has a sharp-edge, then it is a sword or spear; but if it is rounded, it offers a way out of a crisis, it may, if extended over a river in which we are drowning, be the cause of our salvation. If it is thrown at us with a sharp end, it may be the cause of our death. This is a prime cause of confusion where the rod and sword are concerned, but we should remember that spears usually have bronze or iron tips, as do arrows, and that it is this which does harm, not the wooden rod it is mounted upon. This may sound like splitting hairs, but it is essential that these concepts are absolutely clear in the mind of the magician. Uncertainty or hesitation are prime causes of instability, and in magic it is sometimes better to be totally wrong but sure you are right than it is to be undecided.

The element attributed to the rod in this text is air, and air is usually described as being the element of mind; it is also considered to be closely linked to the astrological signs of Aquarius and Gemini. The first of these signs is used by magicians to symbolise both the elemental air and the eastern quarter of their operating circle, or created cosmos. It is illustrated by the diagram of a man's head, the seat of intellect and vision.

Air representing mind is symbolic of the highest mental faculties man possesses; air can penetrate into the smallest vacant space and fill it, as can intellect if developed. Air carries vibrations in the form of sound, and without air we would be cut off from our main source of communication. Besides sound, air also carries scent, and this aspect is represented by incense in ritual workings. Scent is often overlooked as a factor in man's behaviour, but it is a very powerful influence indeed, and that it is recognised as such is borne out by the vast amount spent each year on perfumes and colognes. Would anyone really pay so much for a tiny bottle if they did not feel that it brought results?

Elemental, or 'inner air' is considered to be a force which is mobile, light, subtle and penetrating. Some schools also describe it as hot and moist, but these attributions, although extremely ancient, are lacking in many respects. The air over the Sahara Desert may be hot, but it is hardly moist. However, if you find that these make sense to you, then by all means use them. The elemental spirits of air are the sylphs, and these are usually visualised as small whirlwinds of energy. Their properties are said to consist of attentiveness, intelligence and brightness. They are reputed to be among the more difficult elemental beings to contact and control. The archangel of the air quarter, with responsibility for the elementals assigned to him, is Raphael, and his main task in this context is concerned with teaching humanity, guiding the inner traveller and also with healing wounds an injuries. Raphael is also archangel of sephirah Hod and we will encounter him in this form when examining that sephirah a little way on into our rod exploration. Raphael in his association with the eastern quarter also symbolises the dawning of inner light and awareness; however, this sphere of his function is more correctly placed in Hod than Malkuth.

A major symbol of air is the arrow, and this is after all, nothing but a rod with feathers attached that it may stay true to its target. We could wish for no better symbol of the swiftness of thought, or the deadly accuracy of a penetrating observation than an arrow. A sword is primarily a weapon of hand to hand combat, more defensive than aggressive, for it is limited to function only in the immediate sphere of the wielder. The arrow however, is essentially a weapon of attack, and has little if any defensive potential. We attack our enemy with a flight of arrows, and if he gets too close we then take up our sword. The arrow is also a weapon of stealth, for it is silent, and may fly from the darkness and strike us down before we are aware of any danger. All these associations confirm the correct attribution of the arrow to the element air. It should also be noted that execution, or more correctly sacrifice, by arrow was frequently chosen as a means of liberating the spirit of divine kings. The end of King William Rufus, slain by an archer under an elder tree in the New Forest, on Lammas Day long ago is but one example which springs to mind.

But perhaps the best, and certainly the largest, examples of rod symbols must be those mysterious standing stones and megaliths that dot the countryside from Ireland to the far shores of Europe and beyond. Most people, if asked, will tell you that they have "some bizarre phallic significance, fit only for savages" or something similar. However, these mighty monuments were not built by savages. They are aligned with great precision, using stones hauled by sheer muscle power over vast distances. The effort it must have taken to construct them is barely imaginable, and that they had deep significance is beyond doubt. Unfortunately, much of that significance has been lost. However, through the careful research of experts in this field it is gradually becoming clear that these stones do indeed have a phallic significance in many cases, but it is not in the least bizarre or crude, but rather sophisticated and highly accurate symbolically. For many of these structures are well executed solar observatories with many hidden messages. Many measure the passing of time, and others seem concerned with drawing down the fertile seed of the sky-father. Much research needs to be done, and many mysteries lie concealed there. Before leaving the majestic stones, the author is reminded of the time he visited a well known group of megaliths in Yorkshire and discovered that they were known locally as the Devil's Arrows, coincidence? To travel further on our Tree journey we must leave Malkuth, and enter the lunar sephirah Yesod once more.

Yesod

There are few secondary rod symbols in the subconscious realms of sephirah Yesod; there are, however, a few very direct ones. Firstly, the moon goddess Diana is frequently depicted with a quiver of arrows; secondly, a major tarot attribution of Yesod is the Nine of Wands. With the Nine of Cups, this is significant; for the Wand and Cup are direct symbols of the phallus and vagina, the sexual organs being the correspondence of Yesod manifested in the microcosm.

One of the titles of Yesod being 'the treasure house of images', we should be very surprised if we failed to encounter all sorts of symbols gathered in the etheric atmosphere of this place, and deep subconscious sexual images are but one of the many aspects featured. We should be careful not to place too much importance on them at the expense of other, more subtle, visions we might experience. Instead of dwelling too long in the realm of reflective images we shall take our leave of Yesod, and pass on to the major seat of rod and air power in the lower sephiroth: the mercurial domain of Hod.

Hod

Sephirah Hod is of the utmost importance to the working magician, for together with Yesod, it forms the prime area of his magical consciousness. The mercurial force of Hermes and the lunar force of Thoth are an awesome combination in disciplined and trained hands. Hod is essentially the sphere of intellect, form building, communication, transport and initiation. The so-called vices attributed to Hod include deceit, flamboyance and an inflated ego. The sephiroth, in fact have no vices; these only manifest when an unstable or underdeveloped character receives an 'overdose' of their force. They do not manifest within the Holy Sephiroth, but in the behaviour patterns of the individual concerned. On reexamining the above list, we can see how well some of the better known magicians such as Levi, Crowley and Mathers, to name but a few, fit the 'hermetic overdose' diagnosis. Aleister Crowley, for instance, was intellectually brilliant, possessed of a scheming wit, grossly flamboyant and promiscuously bisexual, all of which correspond perfectly with the archetypal magician of Hod. The apprentice magician will no doubt be relieved to hear that the initiation of Hod can be obtained without the slightest risk of similar excesses if handled in a balanced and disciplined manner.

The mundane chakra of Hod is Mercury, and it is noteworthy that this god-form is frequently depicted with winged sandals, signifying both his role as messenger and his nature as a being of air. It should also be noted that both Mercury and Venus are extremely bright planets, receiving an intense amount of illumination from the Sun; as such they have always been considered highly important links with God. Mercury as Hod, and Venus as Netzach are directly opposite each other on the bases of the feminine and male pillars of the tree respectively. At first this may seem to be rather odd, but in fact it is a correct attribution. We return once again to the 'sexing' of the sephiroth. In Hod, as in Geburah, we have a female potency behind a male facade, as in Netzach and Chesed we have a male potency behind a female facade, although this is not so apparent in the case of Chesed.

Whenever we encounter sexual terminology on the Tree we must remember that invariably we are dealing with a bisexual form, for pure sexual division does not exist on this side of the Abyss. The balance of sexuality within various forms differs, but unless the form is an image of a supernal potency it must contain both male and female elements.

It is this concept which led the said Aleister Crowley to instigate his 11th degree of homosexual magic, for in so doing he believed that he was formulating an alchemical marriage of air and earth, to counterbalance the fire and water version enacted with heterosexual union. The correspondences used relate the phallus to the Hermetic Wand, and the fundament of the passive partner (usually Crowley in his 'Aly' persona) to the Malkuth or Earth element. The symbology used is technically accurate, but if his diaries are anything to go by, the results obtained left something to be desired. Whether this is due to the idea behind the rites, or the way in which they were executed, is a matter of interesting speculation.

The angel order of Hod are the Beni-Elohim, which roughly translates as 'Sons of God'. The inaccuracy is due to the mixed masculine and feminine plurality. These angelic potencies are primarily concerned with the transmission of divine consciousness. They could be likened to units of scaled down 'God Awareness', ready and willing to attach themselves whenever an opening is made available in a suitable mind. The drive within mankind 'to know God' is a result of inner contact with the Beni-Elohim, but to stand any chance of success we require a trustworthy and knowledgeable guide, and Raphael, archangelic overlord of Hod and the Beni-Elohim, is the very best guide a traveller on this path could hope for. Raphael, the 'Healer of God', is one of the four archangels of the quarters, and his special province is that of the east, air; he is illumination in a 'dawning' sense and symbolises instruction in the hermetic arts. Raphael is frequently depicted with his traveller's staff, a phial of golden healing balm and a quiver of arrows slung across his shoulder. The staff is appropriate to his role as guide of the way, and is also symbolic of strength through uprightness and through following the middle pillar of balance. It may also serve as a balancing rod if held horizontally in the manner of a tightrope walker's pole. Such a pole is an advantage when crossing the sword bridges of life, with Geburah and Chesed on either side and an abyss below. We should not look down, but raise our eyes to the light ahead and trust in Raphael's guidance, for he is a supreme source of aid if we stray from the path, and we should never be afraid to invoke his assistance when the blackness of ignorance or wounds of the spirit threaten to overwhelm us. One of my own inner visions of Raphael concerns his towering form, with staff, lantern and quiver of arrows, guiding me along a treacherous mountain pathway in pitch darkness. This is a useful image, worthy of meditation, for it typifies many aspects of this particular archangel, whose friendship we should certainly aim to cultivate if we are serious in our intention of taking the hermetic path.

The god-name of sephirah Hod is *Elohim Sabaoth*, which means 'God of Hosts', but once again gender causes a few problems in obtaining an entirely satisfactory translation. Possibly a more accurate rendition would read 'Male of Female Goddess of Hosts' but this is equally confusing if you are unfamiliar with god-name derivations, so perhaps 'God of Hosts' is the best all round translation, even if it is fifty percent inaccurate.

This name, like all the sephirothic god-names, is highly important, for it is the primary key to understanding the function of the sephirah. Forgetting the controversial god or goddess part, let us examine the significant 'hosts' section.

This is usually taken as meaning a host in the sense of an army, and to a certain extent this is accurate, for divinity does indeed manifest in Hod through the agency of a host of forms filled with force in the shape of the Beni-Elohim. However, this is far from the whole story, for Hod is also the sephirah of ritual magic, and this is of course, concerned with creating forms for divinity to inhabit, so that abstractions may be concreted to a level where the human mind can attain direct contact with form rather than force. Form is fixed and attainable, whilst force is abstract and fluid and, unless we are functioning at a very high level indeed, is very difficult to accommodate without the risk of overloading our inner 'circuits'. Form and force are the two keywords in this context, for if Hod is form what is force? The answer is the fluid opposite of Hod, Netzach. Once more we see a reciprocal energy-form interchange in operation. The 'blend' of force and form may be found in the half form, half force sephirah Yesod, the treasure house of etheric images.

The forms of Hod take many shapes, and the magician must never confuse these self-made forms with the force that inhabits them, for this would be a grave error. They should be considered as vehicles for force to manifest in, and certainly not taken as divine presences 'in person', as it were. This is a particular danger with Hod. The magician, intoxicated by the god-form he assumes, begins to lose his identity and 'confuses his planes', the result of which is usually his downfall, as may be confirmed if one studies the biographies of famous and infamous magicians, past and present. Major symbols of sephirah Hod are caduceus, the entwined serpents, the apron, the names of power and the winged sandals. Most of these are self-explanatory in the light of the material so far examined, but the caduceus and apron are worthy of brief explanation.

The caduceus is essentially a rod with serpents twisted around it. These serpents are the kundalini serpents of male and female. They are not merely twisted around the rod; they are mating. They symbolise the crossing over of polarity as it appears on the Tree and, to a lesser extent, within human beings. They also symbolise the descent of equilibrated light, and as such are an important image to bear in mind. This symbol may profitably be applied to the Tree as a whole; but with specific relation to Hod, the caduceus symbolised advancement through inner reconciliation of sexual motivations, a similar message to that of Netzach, but from a slightly different starting point.

The apron symbol is rather more obscure, but it is nonetheless a significant one, for it provides a close link with both Egyptian and Masonic ritual symbolism. It is still used within freemasonry of course, and it has a dual message. Firstly, it was used by craftsmen in ancient times, and in particular by architects, who used to keep their plans and diagrams concealed within its pockets (it is for this reason that it is popular in masonic circles); secondly, it is a shield for the genitals (as far as I know this has no connection with freemasonry!). Both of these concepts are intimately linked with Hod and the Hermetic path. In the latter instance, we should note that the magical image of Hod is that of a Hermaphrodite, the very word being derived from Hermes and Aphrodite, Hod and Netzach. Both teach advancement and evolution through inner union of the sexual principals.

To sum up: Hod is a sephirah of illumination through conciliation of opposites. It is also the sphere of the magician, craftsman and architect of inner-world forms in a cosmos of his own making. With this in mind, we may pass from Hod to Tiphareth via the 26th path of illumination.

Tiphareth

Sephirah Tiphareth is a sort of 'Grand Central Station' to the sephiroth located below the abyss. It is, as we have seen, intimately linked with distributing energy to the lower sephiroth, and on our return journey it will prove of equal importance. An excellent exercise that will pay dividends in terms of understanding vital principals of Qabalistic theory is to imagine sephirah Tiphareth as the hub of a giant wheel, spokes radiating outwards. These spokes connect to the visualised eight non-material sephirah, Kether, Chokmah, Chesed, Netzach, Yesod, Hod, Geburah and Binah, all of which are 'seen' with the inner eye in their appropriate Empress scale colours. These Empress scale colours apply to the expression of the sephiroth in the world of Assiah, i.e., the planetary aspect. Hence, Hod would be visualised in a yellowish black, flecked with white; Geburah would be seen as red flecked with black, and Tiphareth itself as a golden amber glowing with dull radiance. You should carefully visualise this 'Wheel of Life' spinning slowly in a void, observing the way in which the sephiroth interact and balance each other out. You should attempt to gain some insight into the way in which the spokes act as 'gravity' preventing the sephiroth from leaving Tiphareth's solar system in miniature, and should recognise that this is an expression of a rod principal in operation.

When you have successfully visualised this system, you should meditate upon the wheel symbol and attempt to gain insight into its various other expressions, such as the Buddhist wheel of life, the eight Celtic and Wiccan festivals and other similar examples. After some time you can extend the exercise to higher regions by changing to the Emperor, Queen and King scales of colours, thereby granting access to the worlds of Yetzirah, Briah and Atziluth respectively. The technique has many interesting variations, from visualisation in simple planetary colours to extending of the wheel into a sphere, all of which offer much scope for meditation and expansion of awareness.

The archangel of sephirah Tiphareth is Michael, supreme commander of the forces of fire-light, and not for nothing is he known variously as the 'Prince of Light' or 'Scourge of Darkness'. He is standard bearer of the Solar Logos, leader of the legions of light. His spear indicates the upright path of the middle pillar, a rod of mercy topped by a point of severity, fire guided by wisdom and compassion. When surrounded by the darkness of ignorance we may call Raphael; when floundering due to inexperience we may call on Auriel; but when in danger from sheer unbalanced evil we can do no better than invoke the protection of Michael and his spear of light. It should be noted that Michael's spear (some systems grant him a sword as his major weapon, but this is erroneous; the sword is a weapon of Geburah and of Khamael in particular) is a rod with a point attached, and before the point was affixed it was a simple staff. In this we gain a clue as to how Michael defeated Samael 'the Venom of God'. Now, Samael has frequently been likened to a serpent, not a serpent of wisdom, but of darkness, and when we visualise this staff as a rough hewn pole with a forked end we gain a valuable clue as to the possible method of his capture. It is important to remember that Michael did not destroy Samael, but merely restricted his range of activities somewhat. Thus, does the rod display its qualities of mercy and wisdom.

We shall now take our leave of Tiphareth, and enter the sephirah Chesed, a place of vital importance if we are to understand the rod principle on the Holy Tree.

Chesed

Sephirah Chesed has several titles, the more prominent being Gedulah - Love and Majesty. These give an accurate picture of the basic compulsion driving Chesed. The spiritual experience assigned here is also clear for it is the 'Vision of Love', love not in a strictly 'earthy' sense, but in the wider sense of 'Love is the Law', the spiritual essence of all love. Chesed is essentially a masculine sephirah, for it is located on the positive white pillar of mercy topped by Chokmah, the all-father.

Chesed is also the first sephirah of the manifested universe, receiving its originating stream from beyond the abyss. As such, it is extremely powerful and represents the formulation of all archetypal ideas, the concretion of the abstract, from total abstraction to nascent form, not form as such, for this does not occur until force has travelled much further down the tree, but something which encompasses the idea of form. This is not easy to explain, but if we say that H. G. Wells, when he wrote of submarines and airships was functioning in a Chesed-like mode of consciousness, the concept might be a little easier to comprehend.

It should be noted at this stage that the sephiroth tend to appear rather differently depending upon whether you are approaching them from above or below. We will deal with this in more detail when looking at the pantacle; but for now we should realise that on the outward journey sephirah Chesed is a place of overflowing energy, nonstop, vital life energy, which if it were not restricted by its opposite sephirah Geburah would by now have swamped the universe with love, mercy, plenty and compassion.

This might sound like a good idea, but in fact it is a state of unbalance, for any force needs a counter to maintain equilibrium. The counter to Chesed is Geburah, and vice-versa. If Chesed were not restricted we should rapidly die of boredom, obesity and sheer lack of purpose. We need the sharp spur of Geburah to drive us on. A good analogy here is that of the child who is allowed nothing but his favourite sweets. He may be happy for a while, but before long he will surely become ill, and his teeth will suffer. We should not risk our teeth, the teeth of Geburah, by overindulging in the sweetness of Chesed.

On our return journey, Chesed is the compassion of experience, the wise old man or woman who has enough wisdom and authority to allow the younger generation the freedom to find out right and wrong for themselves, only applying restrictions when things go too far – a synthesis of Chesed and Geburah applied in the correct manner, not authoritarian, but not weak either. True justice tempered by compassion, the way of the middle pillar.

The mundane chakra of Chesed is Jupiter, and a well-known word derived from his name, 'jovial', sums up his influence rather well. Jupiter is generous, merciful, wealthy and powerful; in short, he has everything most people seem to crave. However, as we have seen, if they were granted their wish in full they would soon discover the drawbacks of such an existence. In moderation, Jupiter is a welcome guest; in excess, he rapidly proves to be a liability, as the 'vices' of this sephirah indicate: bigotry, hypocrisy, gluttony and tyranny, for all are clear symptoms of over-exposure to Chesed.

The angel order of Chesed are the Chasmalim or 'Bright Shining Ones' and as their opposites in Geburah are flames of fission, so the Chasmalim are flames of fusion. The Chasmalim represent the furnace of assembly rather than the furnace of dissolution.

The archangel overlord of the Chasmalim is Tzadkiel and this translates as 'Righteous of God', a fitting title for the archangel of Chesed. Tzadkiel represents 'righteousness' in its purest sense. Not the misplaced 'self-righteousness' displayed by mankind on occasions, but cosmic righteousness in the sense of power applied with wisdom and justice, power correctly managed. This archangel is an agent of divine justice in much the same way as his opposite number Khamael is to Geburah. On the outward journey, Tzadkiel devises our lessons; on the way back he sets our examinations and weighs our progress against our objectives. Have we indeed learned our lessons well, or have we failed during our incarnation to grow in wisdom? Tzadkiel decides. Not for nothing are both Geburah and Chesed sometimes depicted as balance scales resting upon the pivot of a sword. The stern voice of Geburah points to our failings, the merciful voice of Chesed looks at our successes. At some point equilibrium will be reached, or a decision made, one way or the other. We either graduate with honours, thereby breaking out of the wheel of life, or return once more to the nursery school!

The major rod symbols of sephirah Chesed are the shepherd's crook and the sceptre of kingship. The shepherd's crook of course is merely a rod surmounted by a ram's horn. We have already seen that this is symbolic of life and regeneration. Hence, the crook is the supreme symbol of mercy applied in a positive sense, and of the wisdom of divine power as it rotates the wheel of karma.

We should also note that Chesed is often termed 'The Sphere of the Justified Ones' and that much emphasis is placed upon the presence of images of saints or 'Hidden Masters' within this sephirah. These are, according to hermetic lore, the highly developed individuals who have made the sacrifice demanded in Tiphareth but instead of passing to the Supernals beyond the abyss remain of their own choice in Chesed within range of humankind to act as mediators and translators of divine force. To anyone developed to such a degree this is a far more painful sacrifice than that of Tiphareth, and it is certainly far harder to sacrifice your own development than it is to lay down your physical life. This latter is a step upwards; the sacrifice of spiritual advancement for others is on an altogether higher level.

The second major rod symbol is the sceptre, seen in the magical image of Chesed held by a benevolent king of great age. This is encompassed in the alternative title of Chesed, 'Majesty'. This king is throned, not riding a war chariot, because his kingdom is at peace, and he rules over an ordered and stable realm governed by the law of love and mercy. Another Chesed symbol is the equal-armed cross, symbolising unity and balance within the houses of the elements, and this is sometimes mounted upon the orb, the symbolism here yielding much to meditation.

A final symbol of Chesed is the mystical stone of kingship. This is sometimes known as the 'Stone of Destiny' and was the means by which power was confirmed upon candidates for kingship in ancient times. It also featured in the various tests applied to would-be kings, the case of Arthur's sword in the stone being but one of the better known examples. The stone symbol occurs all the way along this path, from the ashlar, or cubic stone of Hod, to the mighty phallic standing stone of Chokmah, where we end our quest for the rod or wand upon the Tree.

Chokmah

In Binah we found the great sea which was the source of our magical cup; now in Chokmah we find the fount of our rod and wand symbol. Whereas Binah represents the Great Mother concept, Chokmah represents the Great Father archetype - not archetypal in form, but in force. The English title of Chokmah is usually given as 'Wisdom', but this must not be confused with the wisdom of learned knowledge, such an accomplishment being allocated far lower down the tree in Hod; instead this 'wisdom' relates to the absolutely correct application of force, the force in question being that which both created and drives the entire universe. So it is clear that here, in Chokmah, we are dealing with absolutely vast amounts of raw energy.

There is no simple planetary attribution to Chokmah; the mundane chakra is listed as the entire zodiac. This is not as confusing as it might appear, for what is the zodiac but a series of twelve stations encompassing the attributions of the rest of creation? This symbol, confusing at first, is now clear, for Chokmah is the father of all because it encompasses all. The stars are jewels in the crown of the creator. This is symbolically quite accurate, for a crown is a circle, and when we note that the angel order of Chokmah are the Auphanim, which means 'Wheels' or 'Encirclers', we gain some impression of the cyclic energy state represented by Chokmah. The Auphanim are governed by archangel Ratziel, the 'Herald of God', and it is supposed in legend that he possessed a great book which held the secret of the stars. This is fitting for the archangel of a sephirah with the mundane chakra of the zodiac.

Chokmah is also the sephirah of the 'unpronounceable' name of God, *Yhvh* or the Tetragrammaton. This is best viewed as 'The Big Bang', which heralded the creation of the universe - the voice of creation which uttered the word: sounds and words were very important keys to unleashing power in the eyes of the ancient mystery traditions, as they are to present-day magicians. *Yhvh* is the essence of the 'push' that set the cosmic ball rolling, the influx of positive force that precedes reaction. The phallic symbolism of Chokmah is intense, and perhaps the most important symbol of all is the uplifted 'Rod of Power', representing the energised lingam and the dynamic creative force of the initiator of life, not in a low manifestation of sex energies, but in the highest sense of the sexual concept: absolute masculinity and femininity, which exist only in Chokmah and Binah and nowhere else. Chokmah is male in that it pours forth pure cosmic life energy, and Binah feminine in that it receives this, gestates it, then sends it down the Holy Tree to eventual manifestation in Malkuth.

The rod of Chokmah manifests as the mighty standing stone, the peak of the holy mountain, and the magician's wand when functioning at this level. This rod is also symbolic of the spokes of the wheel of cyclic motion, spokes of infinite length, outside the bounds of time or space, for the wheels are the Auphanim, and the motion is that of the universe encompassing all motion from subatomic to inter-galactic and beyond. The straight line, manifested as an inter-stellar spoke in the wheel of the universe, is perhaps the best example of true divine wisdom one could hope to find, as it represents instantaneous extension to everywhere by the shortest and most direct route. It also links all things to a central hub, a point of perfect equilibrium, where time, space, motion and energy are annihilated by the blinding light of perfection.

The spiritual experience of Chokmah is theoretically the Vision of God face-to-face, the emphasis being on 'theoretically', for no incarnate human in his or her right mind would claim to have had such an experience. The very few claims of this sort that are made are generally the result of Yesodic visions mistaken through ignorance for something altogether different. It is almost certain that such an experience would be a non-survivable event as far as humans are concerned. Without becoming exceedingly abstruse we can explore no further in Chokmah; after all, we are merely examining some principles governing the weapons of magic, not analysing some of the most complex aspects of Qabalistic doctrine.

Before leaving the rod symbol altogether, however, let us survey the things we have so far discovered about it. Our rod is a standing stone, a magician's wand, a pen, a ruler, a maypole with phallic overtones, a sundial and a human spine. It is interesting that both the maypole and human spine are included at this point, for the maypole is encircled by black and white ribbons in a spiral fashion, and the human spine by the coils of the kundalini serpent. Both symbols signify aroused sexual currents; both have spiral forms around an upright rod. Is it another coincidence that it is exactly this energy form which experienced dowsers report in the vicinity of many megalithic standing stones? We return once again to stones and serpents, rods and sexual currents. Thus do we complete the cycle of the rod upon the Holy Tree of life. With a little wisdom and knowledge perhaps we can penetrate the clouds shrouding the symbolism of the holy mysteries, and thereby gain both wisdom and understanding in a wider sense. For now we must leave the rod, and set out once again on the trail of the tools of the magical art. The weapon we now seek is the mighty sword of dissolution.

4 THE SWORD ON THE TREE

So far we have examined the water and air weapons. We now meet the other weapons, which in our system of attributions are represented by the sword and knife. As with the air wand, we find a large measure of conflict between various traditions on the matter of this attribution. Some groups draw no distinction between the sword and the knife, placing them under the government of the same element, which may be fire or air, other groups place the sword as a weapon of Geburah and fire, and the knife as a weapon of Tiphareth and air! All very confusing, and all entirely unnecessary, for a system does exist which provides satisfactory links for these weapons, and what is more, it is accurate in both an historical and symbolic sense.

However, all of these attributions have been found to work in practice, and provided you are able to make the required inner connections to program your 'inner world computer', to yield and correct responses upon the weapon stimuli being applied, you are assured of a workable system. Much of this confusion is related to the purely arbitrary methods many groups, orders and authors have used when placing the weapons within their symbolic framework.

Whilst the basic intuitive link is of vital importance, it is also fallible, and unless it can be verified by other methods is of questionable value to a working group. The lone practitioner may well find his intuitive attributions entirely satisfactory, but it is highly unlikely that an entire group of people will be able to make such a total identification with a set of symbols based upon one person's intuition unless it can be backed up with 'solid' evidence. The reason for this is quite simple. Absolute, total faith and knowledge of the inner message of each weapon is required. True, when working with basic elemental forces it is possible to get by without such complete understanding. When working with higher energies, however, the danger of a muddled and confused system of correspondences cannot be over stressed. If we are to function with effectiveness and security on inner levels, it is vital that we do not get our own 'hot and cold' inner waters mixed! The easiest and best way of avoiding this is to have watertight inner connections, and a solid factual basis for our attributions. This dealt with, we can now look at our sword in Malkuth.

Malkuth

A sword or dagger is born of the action of fire on iron. Before iron was smelted for the first time, knives consisted simply of skilfully shaped pieces of flint, formed to a sharp cutting or scraping edge by striking against other pieces of flint. This too produced sparks, and not only yielded excellent weapons and household implements, but also provided the means whereby the fire might be kindled. The importance of fire to our ancestors cannot be over stressed; fire was literally life or death. Not only did it cook, but it warded off beasts and provided heat, light and a comforting and friendly presence. The fire was revered as a living thing, for not only was it born but in order to live it needed feeding and protecting before eventually dying. It was also capable of becoming angry, and woe betide the person who caused the fire spirit to get upset. It must be placated or the whole tribe's survival was in danger.

Today, we no longer believe such things, but we still speak of burning with 'holy fire' and light 'eternal flames' in honour of great events or people. We still respect fire. The modern magician or witch still deals with these long forgotten fire spirits, and knows them as 'Salamanders', elemental beings who typify the nature of fire. The magician considers elemental fire as active, male, positive and energetic. Fire is the 'drive' which forces us to strive for domination, power or success. This is not strictly true of course, for these things are also closely linked with Earth; but without fire we would stand no chance of 'winning through' and obtaining what we desire. On more subtle levels, fire is the impregnating force, which as lightning struck the primeval oceans and set the chemistry of life in motion. Fire is many things; it is the fire of passion, the fire of vengeance, the fire of will and the fire of illumination. It is in this last context that most magicians contact their 'inner fire' - at least to begin with, for fire is an element which needs to be strictly controlled if it is to be handled with safety.

The archangelic intelligence and overlord of the fire elementals is Michael, who is also the ruler of the solar sephirah Tiphareth. Michael signifies the very best aspects of fire light and is the means by which humans can contact their inner fire without too much risk of getting burnt. Michael is balance, reason and wisdom. Without such limiting factors, fire, which warms us when we are cold, may run away in uncontrolled fission and cremate us. We shall meet Michael again when our journey leads us to Tiphareth, but our first port of call after leaving Malkuth is sephirah Yesod, where an interesting fire link awaits our examination.

Yesod

The angel order of this sephirah are the Aishim or 'Souls of Fire' in English. Some authorities incorrectly attribute the Aishim to Malkuth, but this is undoubtedly an error, for the angel order of Malkuth is clearly the Kerubim. Any attempt to interchange these attributions reflects either a lack of knowledge or a deliberate desire to confound. In some cases this latter is plainly the only reason for certain writers to state what they must realise is inaccurate. What possible advantage could there be in attempting to conceal such a fact? The Aishim are agents of fertility, not only physical but mental, and to grant a non-initiate the keys to contacting them was more than many early writers could bring themselves to do. Their misleading statements that the Aishim were related to Malkuth and the Kerubim to Yesod have since been propagated, both knowingly and unknowingly, by other writers on the same theme.

There is an extremely important link between the Aishim and the Holy Ghost, manifested in the 'Akasha' or astral light of Yesod. Dion Fortune in her excellent book *"The Mystical Qabalah"* neatly evades any detailed discussion of this aspect, despite several alluring hints. However, it is possible to piece together much of the esoteric lore concerning this link by comparing traditional sources with contemporary writers. The best way, however, is to experience this aspect of Yesod yourself by personal workings directed to such an end. This is not work for a complete beginner, for the force under discussion is a potent one, but it is the only way to reach any sort of genuine comprehension of an otherwise difficult topic.

The archangel of Yesod is of course Gabriel, and at this stage it may prove helpful if we translate his name into English. Gabriel means 'Strong One of God' and one of his tasks was to destroy the children of the 'Watchers', reputed to be the sons of Satan.

This, as we know, is a reference to Binah and Saturn. We have already traced the Yesod-Binah link in some detail, but now we find another facet exposed to view. How were these 'bad angels' overcome? By the agency of 'good angels' - the Aishim under the direction of Gabriel; the 'Souls of Fire' sterilising the anti-life elements personified by the 'Watchers'. This is a classic case of fire in its most beneficent mode, as would be expected where it is harnessed to the service of Gabriel and to life.

A second fire link of Yesod is the ram's horn symbol of Gabriel's sacred chalice of life. As any astrologer will tell you, the ram's horn is a clear symbol of Aries, a primary fire sign. This particular aspect of the horn is important in understanding some of the sexual magic operations attributed to both Yesod and the 'Holy Ghost', for it represents both fire and water in one. A true alchemical marriage, and the basis of many hidden rites within the ancient (and a few modern) mystery schools. Other links exist also. To give just one example, Thoth the Egyptian lord of magic, was regarded both as a lunar god and also as 'The Master of Maat', or lord of justice. This is an interesting title, for one important symbol of Maat is a pair of scales, and one of Gabriel's own lesser known symbols is also a pair of scales. It should also be noted that justice is essentially a fire attribution, and has very little, if anything, to do with the water correspondence normally allocated to Yesod - further proof that the simplistic system used by many occultists is sadly lacking. This particular link also ties in with the hidden sephirah Daath, but that is beyond the scope of this present work. For now, we take our leave of Yesod and arrive in Netzach, where we once again pick up the trail of the sword on the Tree.

Netzach

A great deal of the Netzach symbolism was explored when tracing the path of our water chalice, and we must now re-examine this in the light of the reflected fire of Geburah.

One of the symbols associated with the fire aspect of Netzach is a blood red rose. This rose is frequently depicted with a golden, or silver dew upon its innermost petals and is assumed by some to represent the Venus or love aspect of Netzach. In fact, it is a key to understanding the sex-blood-sacrifice attribution, which is the initiated view of Netzach, the rose being symbolic of the blood of the divine king, the dew the vital life energy this contained and the dew upon the rose the release of this energy through sacrifice. This combination is interesting, for the cup and dagger combined indicate a female-receptor and a male-releaser of the blood-energy - the priestess, the sacrificial knife and the blood of the divine king. We are. in fact, speaking of a primitive (in the sense of 'raw') Holy Grail. This may appear to be a barbaric custom, but if you take the trouble to understand the operation from the viewpoint of those peoples of long ago who practised it, it makes a good deal of sense.

The blood-sex link is a powerful one, and it is one which has been used for many thousands of years by many different cultures. What is now regarded as a 'kinky' perversion was once one of the most sacred rites in primitive liturgies; the slaying of the divine king, sometimes at the moment of orgasm, as a means of releasing the vital life energies for reception into the priestess, and thence to the people. Fortunately, such rites are no longer demanded, the modern occultist having developed much more refined methods of obtaining similar ends. However, at one time they were used in times of great need and were doubtless held to be effective. Had they not been so considered it is highly unlikely, that they would have persisted as long as they undoubtedly did.

Not only human sacrifices were consecrated to similar objectives; in some circumstances animal offerings were also favoured. It should go without saying that such rites have no place today, but it is important that we make an effort to understand the symbolism involved. It is interesting to note that the victim is almost always stipulated in associated myths and legends as being male; very few instances of female sacrificial victims are evident. Why this should be so is clear if we remember the male-active, female-passive pattern found in folklore, mythology and the occult doctrines of various traditions. The blood of the male carried the vital positive life energies for reception into the female, who drew upon this current to enhance the 'life spirit' or totem of the group or tribe of which she was guardian. On occasions she would be physically impregnated during the rites and the resulting child, if male, would be hailed as future divine king. The animals most desirable for such rites were those of outstanding strength, courage or virility such as boars, bears or goats. Of course if an animal sacrifice was used, the sexual part of the operation would usually be undertaken by a priest 'possessed' by the spirit of the victim. On occasions where a human victim was used, the sexual part depended upon the willingness of the victim to participate - there is no evidence that the victims viewed this as anything other than a great honour and went perfectly readily to their deaths.

The Mars-Geburah-Fire influx to Venus-Netzach-Water is one which holds many concealed messages if only we take the trouble to look for them. A clue to one of the ancient mysteries, the significance of the number seven, a sacred number in many cultures, may also be found hidden in sephirah Netzach. Not only is this number the prime number of the sephirah itself upon the Tree, but it is found lurking almost everywhere one looks within the mythologies associated with it. The seven stringed lyre of Orpheus, the seven stars of the Pleiades, the seven chakras of

Tantra, the seven branched candlestick of the King of Zion, the seven Rishis of Hinduism, the seven days of the Christian creation myth and numerous other septenary linked mythologies have close ties with various aspects of Netzach. Some of these links are exceedingly obscure; others, such as the tradition of the seven sisters of the Pleiades as doves, comparatively clear. In each case, however, the link can be made, and can provide much useful material for subsequent meditation. Venus as the scarlet woman, exalted over Taurus, is another important association of Netzach, and once again this image will yield much to meditation. Many of the themes encountered here are too involved for discussion in our present context but will, if explored in detail, reveal many recondite aspects of the cup-dagger interaction to the dedicated student of high magic.

To further trace our dagger and sword upon the Tree, we must now leave Netzach for Tiphareth, where a different sacrifice is demanded of us. Before turning our back on Netzach, however, we should note that the god-name of the sephirah is *Yhvh Sabaoth*, the male-positive fire aspect of Elohim Sabaoth, the god-name of Netzach's polarised opposite, Hod. This, too, has an important lesson to teach if we open our inner ears and eyes to it, for the lamp of initiation burns brightly in Netzach.

Tiphareth

Tiphareth is the central hub of the Tree system, and like the sun, with which it can be profitably compared, it represents a strong fire-light force of illumination. Beneath the blazing sun of Tiphareth, stationed directly upon the middle pillar, lie the lunar sephirah Yesod and the terrestrial sephirah Malkuth, Yesod receiving the rays from Tiphareth, then reflecting them down in diluted form to Malkuth. From an astronomical point of view, of course, if Tiphareth were a physical sun, it would be totally eclipsed by the moon of Yesod and the Earth of Malkuth would be in total darkness. The only light would be that reflected off Hod-Mercury or Netzach-Venus. Above Tiphareth on the middle pillar we find only the concealed sephirah Daath and the divine illuminator Kether, this last representing blinding light of such intensity that anybody approaching it would be destroyed by its radiation. Only when no material resistance to its radiant energy is offered is approach possible. The principle here is similar to that used in space research, where it is essential to protect delicate equipment from intense heatwaves. If a dense obstruction is placed between the heat source and the object this merely absorbs so much radiant energy that it begins to act as a radiator and eventually it burns up. On the other hand, if a thin reflective foil is placed between the heat source and the object this is far more successful. It absorbs minimal energy, and consequently does not overheat. The best solution of all is to make the object itself 'invisible' to the radiating source. This can be achieved in a number of ways, but the usual solution is to use a material which offers minimal resistance to the radiations, thereby allowing them to pass through with minimal absorption and consequent overheating. If we wish to approach Kether we must endeavour to achieve the same effect, for to attempt approach whilst offering resistance to its divine emanations would be as suicidal as attempting reentry into the Earth's atmosphere at high speed on an incorrect trajectory with no heat shield. The functions of Tiphareth and Geburah are to reduce us to a pure state, so that we might eventually approach Kether without risk of burning up.

Tiphareth, in some senses, is to the Holy Tree what a nucleus is to an atom. Like an atomic nucleus, it too symbolises pure radiant energy and potential. Like an atom it can save us or destroy us. It is all a matter of application. The light of Tiphareth, however, is inner light, the light of divine illumination and this is possibly even more potent than atomic energy, and equally as dangerous and destructive if invoked without due care and attention. There are too many 'illuminated' fanatics in this world, with their own supposed direct line to God, without occultists swelling their ranks! Such illumination is of course self-defeating, and not in the least divine; often the motives of the person were originally worthy, but the soul-spirit inhabiting the body simply could not stand the intense divine light energy and promptly blew a fuse! Chaos instead of harmony is a frequent result of applying too much power too soon, and nowhere is the risk greater than with fire-light potencies such as Tiphareth or Geburah.

Tiphareth is frequently referred to as the 'Christ' centre of the tree, and this is true, though not at all in the way many people think. Perhaps the term 'Christ' in this context is misleading, for this does not signify Jesus Christ in person, but any resurrected and redeeming god-form, of which Jesus Christ is but one of many. One could equally well call Tiphareth the 'Osiris' centre, but it is better not to personify the force by name at all, and in this manner the danger of overloading on one god-form can be neatly sidestepped.

The archangel of sephirah Tiphareth is Michael, who is sometimes depicted as holding a sword. While this would fit in nicely with our designated fire symbolism it is undoubtedly an error, at least in terms of the Qabalistic system. The spear is beyond doubt the correct symbol for Michael, embodying as it does both the staff of Chesed and steel point of Geburah and symbolising the concept of severity guided by mercy and compassion.

The frequently encountered rose-cross image of Tiphareth is symbolic of a higher vision of sacrifice. The rose superimposed on the sacrificial cross of Calvary is not only applicable to Jesus Christ, but also to Osiris and Dionysus, to whom the magical image of Tiphareth is equally applicable. This magical image is revealing, for it consists of a child, a king and a sacrificed god, a pattern found in so many mythologies attached to redeemer deities. The rose of spirit blooms against the harsh and dense background of mundane matter; the child is born of divine intervention, is hailed as king, is sacrificed in the cause of the divine Great Work, is risen and assumed back to whence he came. The myth and reality are the same for Lord Osiris Onnophris, the 'Justified One', as it is for Lord Jesus Christ the Redeemer, for both are god-forms created by man for the same force to inhabit. This is a seemingly perverse twist to the usual 'God created Man' theme, but is perfectly accurate, for man has created the forms god is perceived as, and in this 'Man created God'. What is a god who is not worshipped, or a man who has no god to worship? Both are incomplete. But of course we are speaking here of god-forms and not of the ultimate god-force, which lies far above these representations. The title of Tiphareth Zoar Anpin, the 'Lesser Countenance', throws a good deal of light on this if taken in conjunction with the title of Kether, Arik Anpin, the 'Greater Countenance'.

Thus, Tiphareth is here conceived of as Kether on a lower arc, a source of divine spirit, not at the well head of creation, but centrally located on the river of life between Kether and Malkuth. This can also be considered as Kether the Father, Tiphareth the Son and Yesod the Holy Ghost, the trinity on the middle pillar. If we think of Kether, Tiphareth and Yesod as the coils on a transformer, we get a fairly accurate image of what is happening. The high voltage is applied at the primary, Kether, the lowest voltage manifesting in the secondary at Yesod. Tiphareth, in the terminology of electronics, is a 'centre-tap' delivering a balanced output midway between the extremes represented by Kether and Yesod. It is impossible to overstate the importance of this, for it represents the most direct path of the descent of Light. At full voltage the light of Kether is limitless, and of unimaginable intensity; it passes to Tiphareth, where it is reduced to the light of the sun, harmonious and balanced, and finally to Yesod, where it manifests in the silver light of the moon, reflected in the psychic waters of the astral plane, the glowing flames of illumination, the Aishim, to end eventually in a moonbeam on Malkuth, the palest reflection of the force encountered in Kether. We can look upon a moonbeam, but the light of Kether would result in our utter destruction, hence the need to transform it to levels capable of co-existing with physical life forms.

We have said that the sacrifice of Tiphareth is of a different order to that demanded of us in Netzach, but sacrifice itself is not as commonly perceived by the uninitiated, i.e., merely giving up something held in high regard. It consists of diverting and transmuting vital energies (never objects) that could be used for self-advancement to other less selfish ends. In the case of sephirah Netzach, this would consist of vital life energies, whereas in Tiphareth it is the release of the energising spiritual essence contained within the Inner Grail.

In the case of a divine king, this reservoir of spiritual energy may be considerable and touch a great many lives directly.

So far in our fire weapon search we have encountered the dagger rather more frequently than the sword; it is only now as we leave Tiphareth and enter Geburah that for the first time we are confronted by the mighty sword in all its fiery glory.

Geburah

There is an unfortunate tendency in some quarters to regard this sephirah as evil, or at least not quite 'nice'. This is a fundamental error, which merely demonstrates the appalling lack of understanding prevalent in some circles. The situation is not helped by astrologers who label Mars a 'malefic' and by fringe occult writers who see in Geburah the embodiment of wanton destruction. The truth of the matter is that no sephirah can be considered good or evil; they are 'good' when balanced or 'evil' when unbalanced. This applies to Tiphareth or Geburah as it does to the rest of the sephirothic ladder. As the sephiroth on the divine Tree are balanced natural emanations of divine force it is physically impossible for them to be 'evil' as long as that state is continued. The klipothic mirror image of the Tree is an unbalanced, hence 'evil', reflection of the normal Tree and is representative of a state of disorder and chaos as opposed to order and harmony. The klipothic Tree is merely the other side of the coin.

The first thing that strikes the enquirer into Geburah is its martial symbolism. The colour red abounds, as do swords, war chariots, flames, smoke, iron chains, scourges and a host of similar attributions, equally severe and warlike. Severity and discipline are, in fact, vital keys to unlocking the mystery surrounding Geburah, which is stern in the way in which it applies the Holy Law, and severe in the way it eliminates transgressions. The war chariot of Geburah is an essential counterbalance to the over-generosity of Chesed, a vital limiting factor preventing an overflow of klipothic force. We can go so far with mercy and generosity, but at some point it becomes necessary to proclaim "Stop! This time you have gone too far!" That voice will be the stern, but just, war cry of Geburah.

The most important thing to bear in mind is that Geburah is the strong right arm of active justice in its most literal sense, not what frequently masquerades as justice in the everyday world. This is more often than not a desire for revenge, itself a klipothic reaction. This is entirely alien to the nature of divine justice, which seeks to correct rather than merely punish. That the correction procedure may be painful is not to be denied, but this is incidental rather than intentional, as would be the case if so-called divine retribution were the motive. This whole concept of divine retribution is an erroneous one, based upon the premise that God is as petty minded and bigoted as many humans. The magician acknowledges only one law, and that is to discover the divine will and follow it absolutely. Believing that all things encompass divinity, he or she seeks for this within, and when he attains to conversation with his Holy Guardian Angel, or inner contacts, he devotes himself entirely to the Great Work and the execution of Divine Law. The devotion to the Great Work is made in Tiphareth, the execution of it enforced by the sword of Geburah. The famous "Do what thou wilt shall be the whole of the Law" dictum sums up this approach perfectly. It is not, of course a licence to commit mayhem and anarchy at the slightest whim, but instead represents a formula for invoking divine order and cosmic justice where previously chaos ruled.

The supreme symbol of Geburah-Mars is the sword which can be usefully regarded as a surgeon's knife, removing the unhealthy tissues with as little incidental damage as possible. If the corruption is beyond salvation, then the mercy of Chesed may act via the sword of Geburah and extend the ultimate mercy of a clean death. For where healing through removal of diseased tissue is impossible, dissolution and subsequent reassembly in a new form is usually the best answer. Although it may be difficult at times, we should never forget that the sword of Geburah is two-edged, that it dissolves only to provide the raw material for eventual reconstruction. This is cosmic recycling on avast scale and is akin to demolishing an ugly, redundant edifice and using the very same stones to construct a magnificent new building where once there was merely an ugly ruin. The material remains the same, only the form is altered. Thus the phoenix is an ideal symbol of the sword of Geburah, which brings not total annihilation but merely temporary demolition.

The sword of Geburah may also prove a friend when we are tied down or held back by bonds better severed. What better way of obtaining release than to take up the sword and with one mighty sweep slash through those bonds we no longer wish to retain? If the ties are truly no longer required, and we earnestly seek to be rid of them, we shall feel little or no pain during this operation, just relief. But if the ties are prematurely severed or if we attempt to hold on to them whilst the sword is at work we risk getting cut ourselves. We should not invoke the sword without full realisation of the possible consequences. The sword can only cut us if we offer resistance; if we offer no resistance we shall be unharmed. Where the earth pantacle is our supreme shield, the flaming sword of Geburah is our best defence if undesired influences gain a foothold.

The angel order of Geburah are the Seraphim or 'Fiery Serpents' in English. The Seraphim represent the operational aspect of fire, as their opposite numbers in Chesed represent the operational aspect of light. Although the Seraphim have destructive potential, they also function as purifying agents on a grand scale. The function of the Seraphim is to bring heat to bear whenever ordered to do so by their overlord, the archangel Khamael, who is responsible for planning their work programme. The Seraphim do not make the decisions, but when instructed are diligent workers. Aleister Crowley once described the Seraphim thus, *"On their heads the triple tongues of fire, their glory like unto the Sun, their scales like burning plates of steel... Upon the storm and roar of the sea did they ride in their glory"* which is an interesting and revealing description, for not only does it contain crystal clear references to the martial sephirah Geburah, but also indicates the close link between the Seraphim and Binah, as symbolised by the stormy sea.

Khamael is the archangelic intelligence of sephirah Geburah, and his name, 'The Burner of God', is descriptive of both his nature and the work he is concerned with. Michael is the ruler of fire-light, but Khamael is undisputed king of fire-heat. Khamael directs the energy units of the Seraphim under divine instruction from Elohim Gibor, the god-aspect of Geburah, which translates as 'God of Battles', although, as we have stated previously, this should really read 'Goddess of Battles', for Elohim Gibor and Mars are essentially feminine forces. The upright sword at Tiphareth symbolises the fulcrum of a pair of cosmic balance scales, with the rod of Chesed in the left hand, and the flaming sword of Geburah in the right. Meditation upon this symbol will teach the necessity of using the sword and rod as equal partners in magical workings, and to be cautious of excesses in either direction.

The 'Grand Sword of Conjuration' and the 'Elemental Dagger' partake of the same basic nature, fire, but are used in entirely different circumstances. The changeover in function takes place half way up the Tree in Tiphareth, where the sacrificial and elemental dagger is exchanged for the sword of power. There is much available in the way of instruction for manufacturing this sword of power in numerous mediaeval grimoires. However, apart from the fact that it is to be used for 'quelling rebellious spirits' little is said about its precise mode of operation.

It should by now be clear that simply making, or buying, a sword, dagger, cup or wand and performing a half-understood ritual over it does not render it instantly magical. A true magical weapon is conceived on inner plain levels and is given physical birth in Malkuth more as a convenience to the magician than for any other reason. A physical sword, wand, cup, dagger or pantacle has no effect on inner levels whatsoever unless it has an independent existence at the levels where it must operate.

It is possible to create a weapon in Malkuth and construct an inner plane reality for it, but the usual evolution of a genuine magical weapon is from the inner planes to physical manifestation, rather than vice versa. This is why simply copying the weapons described in this book will prove ineffective unless you are able to make the required inner links and receive your own inner plane guidance on their unique natures and functions. For no two magical weapons are exactly alike; each has an independent personality, for want of a better word. Really powerful weapons may even have an independent inner plane guardian attached to them serving to protect and oversee the weapon's correct use. Any attempt to pervert the weapon would result in the activation of the guardian, with dire results to the person of anyone foolish enough to attempt to interfere with their divine purpose. The tale of the 'Sorcerer's Apprentice' is fictional, but nevertheless reveals a worthwhile lesson to anyone contemplating dabbling with potencies they do not understand and are unable to control!.

The sword of Khamael is not granted to the magician until he has achieved a certain grade, and with good reason, for such a weapon in the wrong hands could prove disastrous not only to the magician but to those with whom he comes into contact. The karmic repercussions in such a case would be terrible to contemplate, hence the newcomer is advised to delay constructing this weapon until well experienced and able to deal with the possible consequences. This is not said to discourage the neophyte, but to help protect him from him or herself, for the first person an out of control weapon will turn on is the magician involved. This may sound rather melodramatic, and doubtless there will be some who will disregard such advice. Those that get burned will have only themselves to blame.

That said, we now take our leave of Geburah and set out on the 18th path to sephirah Binah, the somewhat surprising source of our fire weapons.

Binah

Our previous encounter with Binah may have misled us into thinking of this sephirah as being concerned solely with water-like functions and attributions, but careful study of the Binah and chalice section will reveal a great many indications of another side to its character - a sea of fire as well as a sea of water. Binah as a fire realm is not as contradictory as it might first appear, especially when the Satan-Lucifer, Venus, destructive mother, Tzaphkiel and Eye of Horus links are taken into account. Another clue is found in the Arthurian legends of the Lady of the Lake, custodian of the mighty sword Excalibur, which rose from her lake and was eventually returned there by Bedivere after Arthur's presumed death. The Hebrew letter attributed to this path, 'Cheth', means a fence, and leading as it does from Geburah to Binah it symbolises perfectly the prevalent forces playing on the path, the result of the energy interchange between the third sephirah Binah and the fifth sephirah Geburah, expressed in the symbol of a chariot which is allocated to this path. Geburah and Binah are very closely linked indeed, and both form an energy circuit of tremendous potency. Both have links with what humans call death, by fire in Geburah, personified by Khamael's sword, the radiant purifying and spiritual fire of greater intensity than any blast furnace, and by the scythe of the 'grim reaper', felling all before it as it scatters the dusts of time in Binah. The Dark Mother and the fiery one cooperate fully!

The tendency to regard death and dissolution as evil is as erroneous as the view that Geburah is evil. Death is essential. Without death the world would be a truly horrifying place to exist in. Life everlasting would be the worst sentence a karmic judge could impose — an eternity of illnesses, old age, boredom on a vast scale, every avenue explored, nothing left to achieve, every thought, experience or emotion jaded through over familiarity. Before long we should pray for death, and for release to another state. An eternity of stasis would be an eternity of insanity; in short, it would be 'Hell'.

A key to Binah is found in the ancient book of formation, the *Sepher Yetzirah*, which describes it as the 'foundation of primordial wisdom' and the 'sanctifying intelligence'. It represents not only the birth of form, but on the return journey the dissolution of form, a return to energy - but a wiser energy than originally set out. In other words, we invariably learn from our life experiences (or should do) and this is translated across the abyss into 'illuminated and sanctified intelligence', not in the sense of knowledge, but in the sense of an understanding of divine law.

Binah is also, at the head of the black pillar, of vital importance in understanding the form building aspects of Hod, although this is straying slightly from our weapon symbolism. Nonetheless we should not make the mistake that because a particular link is not developed in this particular essay it has no relevance. This is most certainly not the case. Hod and Binah are opposite ends of the same pillar, and their importance as a pair cannot be overstated. The magical temple of form in Hod finds its archetypal master in Binah, and even the remarkably confused 'Esoteric Grades' system applies the title 'Magister Templi' to one who has mastered every aspect of form, force and time. It should be added that incarnate humans are incapable of achieving this grade in practice, although that does not seem to prevent some individuals from appropriating the title!

It will be noted at this point by astute students of the Qabalistic system that the path numbers used here, and the Hebrew letters attributed to them are, in certain places, different from those given by certain other writers. It should be recognised that the Tree is a living system, and one which should certainly not be rigid and inflexible. There are as many ways of analysing the Tree and making attributions to its fruit and branches as there are students of the Qabalah. Simply to accept these attributions as the only correct ones displays a flaw not in the system of correspondences but in the student himself. Unless the Tree lives for you, it is impossible to 'live the Tree' in the way it must be lived if real progress is to be made on it. This 'living' does not mean accepting someone else's secondhand correspondences, attributions and descriptions without question; it means climbing the Tree yourself, and discovering your own personal truths. Dogmatic acceptance of other people's beliefs is no way to gain a solid foothold on the branches of the Holy Tree of Life. The present author, by the way, does not wish to see his correspondences and attributions become accepted as the ultimate gospel truth by students. He does wish to see them used initially to gain a foothold, but after that nothing would please him more than to discover that talented students had disregarded them in favour of their own, unique, Tree-key system.

This multiplicity of truths is unique to occultism; it is certainly not encouraged by the established religions, and it is to be hoped that mutual tolerance prevails and things stay that way. Nothing would be worse than for a set of 'Thou shalt believe this' or 'Thou art not permitted to believe that' guidelines to be drawn up and everyone forced into line on pain of excommunication from polite occult society! The attributions and correspondences given here have been tried, tested and not found lacking, but, by all means change them if you feel that you can get better results another way.

To return to Binah. Our sword symbol is encountered directly in this sephirah in several guises. Some pictures of the Virgin Mary ('Stella Maris') depict her with a bleeding heart pierced by three swords. It will be remembered that there are three goddess aspects in Binah and that Binah itself is the third sephirah of creation. Venus, as dark Ishtar, also takes up the sword in Binah, and Venus herself was certainly considered as an evening as well as a morning star. What is even more interesting is that Venus was thought to enter the nether world at times. Astronomically, this is due to the planet's periodic periods of invisibility, but to the ancients it signified her entry into hell. We know that directly below Binah lies Geburah, filled with images that frequently represent an ideal 'fiery hell' by philosophers.

The Venus-Sword link is vital in understanding of the origins of the fire weapons. The biblical image of Moses raising his staff entwined with two fiery brass serpents is most revealing, for brass is the metal of Venus and this demonstrates the Seraphim's traditional links with that planet; the serpent is a symbol of polarity, the essence of both Binah and Venus. The serpents entwined around an upright rod symbolise the middle pillar way of harmony through union and balance of opposites.

Another link of special interest to a working magician is typified by Binah. The triangle of art, the area wherein spirits are manifested during Goetic evocations, has its roots in this sephirah. The Spirit-Triangle-Moon-Binah connection runs thus; spirit is perceived as a primary type of form, the straight line being force; the next development is the triangle, typified by Chokmah and Binah respectively. The moon is a place of astral currents, moreover; it is the realm of the Aishim, the 'Souls of Fire' and the 'Holy Ghost'. The sephirothic geometric sign of Binah is the triangle, and this, most surprisingly of all, is a pyramid of fire. That this should be so is clear if the precise function of Binah is meditated upon. Further confirmation of this will be found in many books on magic, where the Moon-Binah-Triangle link is mentioned, but not elaborated upon, time and again.

Further understanding of the descent of fire on the Holy Tree must come from personal study and meditation, for 'Qabalah' means 'received teaching' in an inner sense. True knowledge of the Tree can only come from personal dedication and effort, not from reading books, and not from accepting another's viewpoint without question. That is belief, not knowledge, and there is a world of difference between the two.

We have now completed our analysis of the sword and dagger upon the tree, and must now set out once more to discover the links connecting the last of our weapons of magic with the spheres of the Holy Tree. The weapon we seek is the pantacle, symbol of Earth and Malkuth.

5 THE PANTACLE UPON THE TREE

The near-universal symbol of elemental Earth in magical lodges is the pantacle, which is usually a disc of brass or wood from roughly 75mm (3 inches) to 150mm (6 inches) in diameter. This is painted or engraved with symbols appropriate to Earth. After our somewhat controversial dealings with sword and wand, it is a relief to gain the solid ground of the pantacle, for like the chalice, there is a good deal of agreement among magicians as to its attributions, correspondences and symbols.

The pantacle is essentially a passive and defensive weapon; it interposes a wall between the magician and hostile forces and provides a firm base for the operation of the other weapons. It seems that the word 'pantacle' is derived from the symbol of the pentacle, the five-pointed star representing the union of the four elements under the dominion of spirit, just as the earth is the physical expression of those same forces. Another common symbol placed upon the pantacle is the hexagram, an ancient and powerful glyph representing the universe.

We begin our examination of the pantacle in Malkuth, sephirah of the elements and of material expression, a place with special significance to the operation of the magical pantacle.

Malkuth

We have seen how the other elemental weapons find their expression in sephirah Malkuth, the water chalice, air wand or rod, and the fire dagger. We now encounter the 'Earth of Earth' aspect of Malkuth in the form of the pantacle: the physical chalice in Malkuth represents the water of earth, the physical wand air of earth, and the dagger fire of earth. Each finds its eventual elemental expression upon the firm ground of the pantacle.

Elemental Earth is the most dense of all the elements; its natural opposite is therefore air, although, as we shall see, it also has close links with Akasha or 'spirit', for it is *"alike unto Kether but after a different fashion"*. This is an allusion to the spirit enshrouded by matter, the mystical reflection of Malkuth to Kether, and Kether to Malkuth, which we shall discuss in some detail further along in our journey.

One of the principal functions of the pantacle in Malkuth is that of a shield. It defends by reflection and prevents penetration. The shield is the true weapon of Auriel, archangelic overlord of Earth, as the spear is the weapon of Michael or the arrows the weapons of Raphael. The weapon of Gabriel is the horn of awakening, a passive weapon like the shield. The horn awakens us to danger, the shield deflects the attack and we then go on the offensive with the active weapons of Michael and Raphael. When we realise that the shield of Auriel is the shield of experience, the horn of Gabriel the instinctive warning voice of self-preservation, the arrows of Raphael the darts of wisdom and the spear of Michael the sword point guided by mercy, we gain a clear insight into the passive and active states of our weapons at archangelic levels of consciousness.

When in danger of attack from disturbing or unbalancing influences or forces, it is to the shield of Auriel we should look for our strongest defence. The erection of a 'shield wall' around us, formed by performing an invoking rite of earth and calling on Auriel in the god-name of Earth, or the names and letters of the Great Northern Quadrangle if working the Enochian system, will suffice to reflect even the most unpleasant currents back to where they originated. This passive form of defence is so effective on magical levels that there is seldom any need for more drastic measures, such as an invocation of the forces pertaining to the sword. The shield method has a major advantage in that being entirely passive there is no possibility of any comeback, a risk which is encountered should an active attack be successfully deflected.

Another vital function of the pantacle is to provide a good solid bedrock for us to base our self-made ladder upon before commencing our climb up the sephiroth toward the hidden summit of Kether. Failure to obtain a firm foundation before setting out would doom an intended ascent to certain disaster before even the first run of Yesod was reached. Such a futile exercise could usefully be likened to building a vast temple of solid stone upon a quagmire. Without the stability which is Malkuth's supreme gift our hypothetical temple, or our genuine inner temple, would both sink into oblivion under a sea of mud. Of this latter example, the experienced occultist is all too frequently reminded, as he sees promising students neglect 'boring' groundwork in favour of more glamorous aspects of magic. Feet of clay tend to reveal themselves at the most inopportune moments. Halfway through a ritual of Goetic evocation is not the best time to discover that you have been inscribing your banishing pentagrams upside down or back to front!

The pantacle is also used in all magical operations where it is desired to produce a material effect from interventions higher up the sephirothic ladder. In this it resembles a communion plate, for upon this disc the force of divinity manifests in physical form. Form inhabited by force - a key phrase where the pantacle and 'earthy' operations are concerned.

The angel order of Malkuth is the Kerubim and it is illuminating to meditate upon their appearance, which is a composite, being composed of an ox, lion, eagle and man, these being none other than the elements Earth, Fire, Water and Air at the level of the fixed zodiacal signs of Taurus, Leo, Scorpio and Aquarius. The Kerubim feature prominently in most forms of ritual magic for they themselves are but lower reflections of the *Chioth ha Kadosh*, the four original Holy Living Creatures of Kether. That these angelic potencies have long been recognised by the priesthood of the Holy Mysteries is beyond doubt, for their forms may be seen in the winged sphinxes encountered all over the far and middle east. Similar Kerubim guarded the 'mercy seat' over the Ark of the Covenant, and further reference to the bible will reveal Kerubim placed at the gates of Eden after the eviction of man.

The Kerubim, representing the holy energies directly behind physical manifestation, are of vital importance to the magician who seeks to control these energies and harness them to the service of the Great Work. The archangel of sephirah Malkuth is Sandalphon, which roughly translates as 'The sound of Sandals'. Unlike most names upon the Holy Tree of Life, this name is of Greek origins and owes nothing to Hebrew. This is more than a little interesting, for the archangel of Kether, Metatron, also derives his name from Greek. This not only suggests a link between the two, but also indicates a later attribution than the rest of the archangelic potencies upon the Tree. In fact the link between Sandalphon and Metatron is more or less total, for they are the same force at different levels of expression. Nowhere is the Hermetic axiom of "As above so below" better exemplified than in the relationship of Kether and Malkuth.

The god-name of Malkuth is *Adonai Malakh*, meaning 'Lord King of the Land'. This is not of course an individual personage, but is the particular aspect of divinity expressed in this sephirah. The lesson *Adonai Malakh* has to teach is that God is present everywhere, even in the grossest form of matter. We should not despise or reject matter, for it encompasses as much divine nature as spirit but after a different fashion. This is a most important lesson, and one which is frequently overlooked. Rejection of material expression entails rejection of the divinity that is concealed within it; matter is but the outer robe of concealment to the spark of spirit within. To further explore our pantacle symbol we must leave Malkuth and enter the lunar regions of sephirah Yesod.

Yesod

One of the titles attributed to Yesod is 'Foundation' and this is reinforced by the god-name *Shaddai el Chai*, meaning 'Powerful' or 'Almighty Overlord of Life'. The archangelic name Gabriel, meaning 'Strong One of God', is also meaningful in the overall context of Yesod once we have realised that behind the fluid waters of the Moon lies a great strength. This may not be apparent at once, but detailed examination of lunar symbolism reveals the concept of the fluidic waters of semi-materialised form being at last organised into physical 'reality'. The spiritual experience assigned to Yesod is 'the Vision of the Machinery of the Universe' - a revealing and illuminating concept. In fact, Dion Fortune made the keen observation that *"if we liken the kingdom of earth to a great ship, then Yesod would be the engine room"*. How simplistic but how very true!

Yesod is a rather confusing place at times, as befits a sort of 'halfway house' between mind and matter; but it is a place of vital importance to the magician, or indeed to anyone intent upon exploring inner realities. Yesod is a receptor of force and in this it resembles a less material version of the earth itself. The forces it receives emanate from the rest of the Holy Tree of Life and before precipitating down to 'final matter' they first pass through the sphere of Yesod for assembly into recognisable forms. If the higher sephiroth represent ideas in the Divine Architect's mind and 'blueprints', then Yesod is the packaging department of our universal factory.

It can be most illuminating to study the relationship of various god-forms attributed to the sephiroth upon the Holy Tree. A time-consuming practice it may well be, but the rewards will more than justify the expenditure of effort required. In the case of Yesod we learn that appropriate god-forms include Shu, Zeus, Diana of Ephesus, The Holy Ghost, Atlas and all three phases of the lunar goddess. Another vital attribution is Thoth as Lord of Moon magic.

This is an interesting collection well worthy of further study and a great deal of meditation. The Shu-Atlas connection is especially interesting, for in the case of both Shu and Atlas we have the concept of a god supporting the heavens upon uplifted arms. His feet rest solidly upon the ground, but the strong one alone supports the arch of the sky. This feat of cosmic strength is especially relevant to the path between Malkuth and Yesod. An absolute wealth of lunar symbolism exists and the keen student of the Holy Mysteries would be well advised to spend some time on original research and meditation in this area, for seemingly obscure lunar connections have a habit of leading to vitally important conclusions.

It is not immediately clear, for instance, how the link between the seventy-two good angels of the *Schemhamphoresch* are linked with Moses, or indeed how Moses himself is linked with Yesod, but some careful detective work in this area will not only reveal the connection, but may open up a whole new area of research to the student.

To seek yet more symbolism connected with the pantacle we must leave Yesod for the last time and enter Hod, the realm of the temple maker.

Hod

When we last visited Hod it was in search of a light and airy principle connected with our air wand, but we must now look closer, for under the drifting air symbolism a very dense and heavy Earth principle awaits our attention.

Hod can be readily summed up as a sphere of concretion, a giver of form to force. We know that concretion and crystallisation are properties of the pantacle and that a combination of thought (air) and form (earth), suggests a union between the wand and pantacle; the magician in his temple, in fact, the force of will moulding the etheric oceans into form. Perhaps the best pantacle link we can find in Hod is that of the Roman Catholic mass, where the god-name of Hod, *Elohim Sabaoth*, 'God of Hosts', takes on a different meaning from the usual 'armies' interpretation placed upon it. In this operation of High Magic, for it cannot be denied that the mass does indeed constitute a magical operation, we have the ensouling of a physical form, the Host, laid upon a platen, a pantacle, by the spiritually invoked force of light in an act of transubstantiation. The 'light' concept is represented by the rod-lance-spear symbol found in Tiphareth as the 'lance to grail' and in Hod as the magician's wand. It is the application of divine spirit to matter. The operation of the mass entails giving form to force, and this is most definitely the form of Hod, the spiritual form of force.

Magically speaking, we must use the pantacle of Hod as a means of materialising unformed energies into forms with which we can deal objectively. We take an abstract concept and crystallise it until we are able to relate to it directly. All god-forms are creations of Hod, man-made envelopes for otherwise abstract divine force.

Much masonic symbolism is related to sephirah Hod and especially with the temple building aspect of the sephirah. The apron which we have already mentioned is of course the sign of the giver of forms, the master mason, wherein he holds concealed his plans and diagrams. Another masonic symbol associated with Hod is that of the unhewn stone, which lies awaiting the craft of the master mason to assume its final perfected form. This can be likened to the neophyte within the temple awaiting the training, discipline and understanding which will enable him to perfect his own self.

Elementally, Hod is frequently attributed to water, as Netzach is attributed to fire. By now it should be clear that such straightforward and simplistic attributions not only fail to display the total picture of the sephirah in question, but also tend to mislead and confound the student. Whilst certain characteristics of Hod do indeed display 'watery' properties, others display 'airy' properties, whilst yet others display 'earthy' or 'fiery' properties. To say that Hod is exclusively one or other of these is a patent falsehood. Hod, like the rest of the sephiroth, is a complex mixture of elemental forces, not merely a two-fold mix such as 'air of earth' or 'water of fire' but as a highly evolved blend of elemental and spiritual forces. It has been said that earth appears for the first time in Malkuth, but this is not in fact the case as the earth principle may even be found in Chokmah. Anything which precipitates toward manifestation displays an earth attribution. While philosophers and esoteric Qabalistic scholars may grapple over the exact blend involved at each stage (even Aleister Crowley contradicts himself several times over in *Liber 777*, the 'bible' of practising magicians insofar as correspondences are concerned) let no one doubt the complexity and subtlety of the Tree so far as elemental forces are involved. Accept the validity of any correspondence only after testing the water with your own toe! And then not as absolute truths but only as aids to evocation or invocation; correspondences are tools, not holy writ. If this week you find Hod rather watery on your astral visit, do not assume that this means it will necessarily be so next time you pass through its portals. Nothing is absolute save the One, and such a concept is far above Hod.

In certain mystery schools it is usual to set initiates a specific task to master before being admitted to a particular grade. It is no secret that the task allotted to Yesod is clairvoyance and the development of the 'Body of Light'. The same curriculum transposed to Hod is the understanding and construction of god-forms and similar telesmatic images.

A telesmatic image is nothing more than a 'tuned resonant circuit' designed to receive 'divine radiations' of a specific frequency. All god-forms are telesmatic images, as are the images of the four elemental archangels invoked when the magician casts his circle or 'builds' his temple. The other task of the initiate of Hod is to absorb the meaning and function of the Holy Names and versicles. Thus armed with the barbarous names of evocation and the ability to construct telesmatic images of considerable potency the initiate may begin to call himself a magician. But let him never forget that the object of his operations and his study is to perform a mass of the Holy Mysteries of Light, infusing himself with the brilliant white light of universal divinity and so become one with it. For much more on the theory and practice of Telesmatic Images see *"The Book of Celestial Images"* wherein their construction and applications are analysed in some detail.

Tiphareth

Tiphareth as the sphere of sacrifice by the Divine King, or God Incarnate, is by now familiar to us. However, not only does Tiphareth represent the route by which the Divine King returns to his heavenly realm; it is also the principal sphere of his manifestation during descent. This represents a far greater sacrifice than any return could possibly involve.

We are continually told that "Jesus died for us". The fact that he was born for us is rarely mentioned, except possibly in connection with the 25th of December each year! This is reflected in the attitude of many hell-fire evangelists, who dwell upon the agonies of the crucifixion to the extent that the mysteries (and contradictions) of the conception are almost entirely forgotten. The magician should ever be aware of such folly for it leads only to klipothic unbalance. When considering the Omega, let him remember the Alpha.

The god-name of Tiphareth is *YHVH Aloah Va Daat* meaning 'God made Manifest through Knowledge', a clear indication of the materialisation of god-force via light, which typifies the character of sephirah Tiphareth at all levels.

To Tiphareth and the illuminating and redeeming power of light is allocated the mysterious keyword I.N.R.I. and the formula of IAO. Most people will be familiar with I.N.R.I. as the phrase "Jesus of Nazareth, King of the Jews", but it has a far deeper meaning to the Qabalist, who interprets it thus:

I = *Yod* = Virgo
N = *Nun* = Scorpio
R = *Resh* = Sun
I = *Yod* = Virgo

Virgo is seen as representing the virginal origin of life, Scorpio the state of death and transformation, the Sun as source of light and life and the final Virgo as resurrection through knowledge of the Light. This sequence is further expanded by the addition of various God form images:

Virgo = Isis, Mighty Mother
Scorpio = Aphophis, Destroyer
Sol = Osiris, Slain and Risen
IAO = Isis, Aphophis, Osiris

The Latin word LVX meaning 'Light' is now woven into this format to produce the following formula:

L = the sign of the Mourning Isis
V = the sign of Typhon and Aphophis
X = the sign of Osiris Risen
LVX = The Light of the Cross

This basic formula is featured in the Golden Dawn's Adeptus Minor Ritual and is perhaps one of the finest rituals extant for invoking the redeeming force of Tiphareth's light as manifested in Osiris or Christ. A second important word attributed to Tiphareth is *Yeheshua*, the Hebrew name of Jesus Christ, formed of the letter 'Shin' representing the fire of the Holy Spirit within the formula of YHVH. This word in itself can form a remarkably effective defence against the forces of darkness, ignorance and evil. And

Yeheshua can be represented not only by the sword or wand but by the pantacle as the solar disc of illumination, shield of knowledge and force of the manifested God.

Tiphareth then, is a sphere of both incarnation as well as sacrificial dis-incarnation. The incarnation sector would relate to the earth path of the pantacle, the dis-incarnation section to the air path of the wand. This is a gross oversimplification of course, but it should give some clear idea of the general concept. Our Tree journey is a two-way affair; before we can die we must be born and we cannot return until we have left.

A final symbol of sephirah Tiphareth, and a most valuable one, is that of a cube, the simplest form of solid. This is an indication of the first crystallisation of form, reflected into Hod, and finally made manifest in Malkuth.

Chesed

We have encountered sephirah Chesed as a place of mercy, generosity and love. We now encounter it on a different basis as the sphere of the formulation of archetypal ideals. Chesed is frequently viewed as an energetic masculine sephirah due to the way in which it outpours divine energy into the limiting sphere of Geburah. However, before it can give, it must receive and this facet of Chesed is regrettably overlooked by some students. It should not be forgotten that Chesed does not generate divine force, but instead receives it from beyond the Abyss in a receptive and feminine mode of operation before transmitting it in a radiating and masculine form. The student is here referred to the *Sepher Yetzirah*, where he will find Chesed entitled 'the Receptive Intelligence'. The Yetziratic texts in general can be recommended for those wishing to interpret the Tree in terms of practical ritual symbolism, for they are a good deal less abstruse and confused than many later expositions upon the same subject.

Descending the Tree, Chesed is the powerful and vital force of youth, the promise of future action. On the return it is the wisdom of age, acquired through doing and trying to do. Chesed has many facets, as do all the sephiroth upon the Holy Tree of Life.

The geometrical form associated with Chesed is the square, the two dimensional form of a cube, previously found in Tiphareth. This is an interesting link, which provides excellent insight into the idea of a cube, before it actually becomes one. Chesed as the first sephirah of the manifested universe represents the formulation of an archetypal idea, the concretion of the abstract into something with the potential for eventual expression as form. This can be further illustrated by considering a river. If the lower sephiroth represent settlements upon the banks of this river, then Chesed represents the spring from which it wells, and Chokmah would represent the rain clouds which themselves made the spring a possibility.

The god-name of Chesed is *EL* or *AL*, composed of Aleph and Lamed. Aleph is usually considered to signify a beginning and one of its symbols is that of an ox. Lamed may be considered as signifying an uplifting force and one of its major symbols is a wing. Formed into a composite symbol we have here an image of a winged ox, a mythical creature with a hidden message, the union of Earth and Air resulting in the inertia of Earth being overcome by the wings of Spirit. The winged ox or bull also symbolises perfectly the pantacle and air wand conjoined, the plenty of the Earth governed by the rod of mercy, which is Chesed's to wield with love. This union of Earth and Air is, however, on an altogether higher level than that found in Chesed's diametrically opposed sephirah, Hod.

It is stated by certain authors that the element assigned to Chesed is that of water. However, once again, this may be viewed as a technical error, for the forces inherent within Chesed are far too complex to be allocated such a simplistic attribution. Each sephirah is the sum of those above it and to stress Binah's influence upon Chesed at the expense of Chokmah's and Kether's is bound to cause a degree of confusion in dealing with its potencies. This is the danger of placing elemental attributions at this level of the Holy Tree, for elemental forces do not exist here in the same form as they manifest in the lower branches, and the use of the term 'elemental' can be misleading in this respect.

A second type of geometrical figure, the pyramid, is also found in Chesed and represents the developed form of the pyramid originated in Binah. However, this should not be taken as proof that the sole originator of Chesed is Binah, for that is patently not the case, even if Binah directly preceded it in the Order of Creation. Out of Binah was born Chesed, but the forces that flow via Chesed find their origination as much in Chokmah as Binah. The specific order of creation has less to do with the type of forces flowing within the sephiroth than some Qabalists seem to imagine. However, all this is open to contention, and by far the best way to discover the truth is to make a regular habit of meditating upon the tree, and to pay visits to the sephiroth in question yourself. This way your personal truth will become manifest within your own reality. For this is the only ultimate truth. The Tree, like life, is what you make it!

Chokmah

We examined many of the attributions and correspondences of Chokmah when researching the origins of our wand. We now take another look as we seek the origination of the pantacle, symbol of

Earth. Any symbols applied to Chokmah, Binah, and Kether are inherently defective, for in reality these regions are far too abstract to relate in any meaningful way to human symbols. We can only attempt to comprehend in a rude fashion their general nature and functions, through the application of even cruder symbols, for it is through symbols that we have our only hope of ever coming in any way to terms with the potencies they represent. What little we can grasp, however, is well worth the intense effort it may take.

Chokmah is entirely unmanifest, like Binah, and if we state that Chesed is the first sephirah of the manifest energies of God, then Chokmah is the place of creation of the sub-atomic particles which form the stream of energy which passes to Binah for processing before 'birth' or 'crystallisation' takes place in Chesed. Even this 'birth' is not a birth of matter but the birth of an idea or archetypal concept, which shows how far Chokmah itself is from human comprehension. Chokmah is the divine motivator behind all creation, not merely physical creation, but creation of Divine Law. In short, Chokmah may be regarded as the sphere of non-physical manifestation twice removed, only one step from positive nothingness. The concepts of positive and negative nothingness, of course, are located in the nil world of god-consciousness found in Kether.

It was in Chokmah that the words "Let there be Light" were uttered, the absolute application of divine force at full pressure. Chokmah is a state of unmanifest force; hence, humans are incapable of either understanding or dealing with it directly.

The major symbol, inadequate though it is, of relevance to Chokmah is the Crown of Creation, which is not part of creation, but the directing force behind it, universal knowledge and wisdom. This crown is related to the pantacle in several ways; both are circular, both represent the plane of manifestation, and both required a positive act of initiation to create. On this basis, if

Chesed is the prototype, Binah is the blueprint, and Chokmah is the idea in the inventor's mind. On the same basis, Kether would be the fact of the inventor's existence in the first place, making all the rest possible. Chokmah is also pantacle-related in that it initiated a trend towards crystallisation, and anything which functions in such a manner, even at such exalted levels as this, is related to the humble pantacle upon the magician's altar.

As Chokmah is the most abstract kind of force, so is Malkuth the densest kind of matter and as such both are intimately related to the other, each being a polarised opposite of the same primal force, expressed in form and force.

Once again the Yetziratic texts are a help in sorting all this out, for they relate Malkuth and Chokmah as expressions of the Inferior Mother and the Superior Father respectively. Because manifestation takes place through the union of opposites, the principle of polarity is implicit not only in the microcosm, but in the macrocosm. It is impossible to imagine anything more abstract and random than a free air molecule in total darkness and zero gravity, or more dense than a neutron star, both with enormous potential energy and both with physical expression in Malkuth and spiritual expression, or more properly, origination, in Chokmah. The magician, with his or her pantacle, wand, dagger and cup, hopes to evoke within his microcosm these macrocosmic forces and hence direct them where he Will. His very thought and every desire is directed toward one end, the completion of the Great Work, the union of matter with spirit under the law of love.

The archangel of Chokmah, Ratziel, in his mighty Book of Stars, details the seventy-two quinaries (spaces of five degrees each) of the zodiac, which as we have seen is the mundane chakra of Chokmah. The *Schemhamphoresch* consists of 72 trilateral names, which yield 72 angelic names and this is of great importance in understanding the nature of Chokmah and even the nature of the archetypal pantacle. Such concepts are highly abstruse and complex in the extreme, proving of interest only to the most dedicated student. Lack of reliable printed matter in itself virtually precludes serious study outside of a properly contacted magical lodge. However, those who feel inclined to develop an interest in this direction could do worse than meditate upon the archetypal image of Moses while calling upon Ratziel for cosmic illumination. Crowley's *"Liber 777"* might also provide a few carefully concealed clues. The *"Goetia of Solomon the King"*, although dealing with different potencies, is also well worth studying in this connection.

Our survey of the major magical instruments is now complete and all that remains is to take a brief look at the less well-known trappings of the magician's craft before setting about constructing them on the physical plane.

6 THE MINOR WEAPONS ON THE TREE

The use of the term 'minor' should not, in this instance, be taken to mean that the items under discussion are in any way unimportant or inferior. Each in its own way is equal to the 'major' weapons. The weapons described here are usually not of a commanding nature; that is to say, they are not used primarily in evocation or to influence any exterior force. They work instead upon the mind of the magician, reminding him or her of the scheme of things and reinforcing the representation in physical form of the inner plane realities behind his temple. Each serves in its own way to prepare the magician spiritually for his work.

The Censer

Elementally speaking, the censer is a combination of fire and air. By means of fire it reduces the gross resins, herbs and oils to that lightest of elements, air, in a true act of transmutation. The censer is also a weapon (or, more correctly, implement) of sacrifice and as such finds its major attribution in sephirah Tiphareth.

The burning of incense is an incomparably ancient form of religious activity, for ever since our distant ancestors discovered that different woods, herbs and flowers made pleasing smells, such substances have found their highest use in worship and magic. One does not have to be a magician to appreciate the vastly different effects offered by various incenses. We are attracted by myrtle, repelled by asafoetida, elevated by frankincense and saddened by myrrh. The ritualist knows the effect of a great many substances when burned as incense, and is aware of the detailed correspondences of each. By their aid he may create a perfect atmosphere for whatever force he chooses to invoke. To give but one instance, to the magician myrrh denotes suffering, sacrifice, Tiphareth and the 'redeemer' god-forms such as Osiris or Christ. The mind of the magician, upon detecting the aroma of myrrh, at once fills with all the correspondences associated with the forces mentioned above, and hence, through the operation of the law of resonance, becomes immediately attuned on inner levels to the reception or transmission of those forces.

The proper use and importance of incense in ritual cannot be overstressed for it is one of the most effective aids at the magician's disposal. Incense burners come in a wide variety of shapes and sizes. For general purposes the best type are those which may be suspended from chains in the manner of a church censer, but unfortunately these tend to be very expensive indeed. Many ritualists opt instead for a burner which stands upon a base instead of being suspended. These are much cheaper and are readily available from occult suppliers and importers of oriental brassware. The best all-round solution, however, is to obtain a high quality standing thurible and convert it yourself to a hanging type swing-chain censer by the addition of suitable chains. If attempting such a conversion be careful of the security of the chains and fixtures, as a poorly suspended censer represents a grave fire hazard.

The Altar

The altar represents the plane of the magician's operations, and is attributed to Malkuth. The usual form of altar is that of a double cube. It is also attributed to Yesod, though after a different fashion, for it also represents the formative world through which the magician works. For this reason the altar top should be devoid of symbols before commencing work. Let the magician fashion his world according to his will. Most magicians make their altars from sheet plywood or chipboard, which can be obtained pre-cut to specified sizes and assembled with wood-screws and glue before giving the whole a coat of matt black paint.

The Ring

The ring represents eternity, encircling and the divine will. It is also related to the wand in that it expresses the will of the magician himself. For these reasons it too finds its roots in Chokmah, Chesed and Hod.

The Lamen

The lamen is related to both Malkuth and Tiphareth for it lies upon the magician's breast, where it is visible only when he lowers his eyes. Yet it carries a message of illumination and reminds him always of the Great Work.

The Lamp

The lamp is attributed to Netzach, where it illuminates through the agency of fire and water. It symbolises the fires of Geburah over the minor seas of Netzach, the force of will over uncontrolled passion. This lamp must not be confused with the lamp of Kether, which is an altogether different symbol.

The Apron

The apron is the symbol of the master builder of forms and as such finds its attribution in Hod, where it manifests as the apron of the master architect of the temple.

The Sandals

The sandals are attributed to Yesod, and to a lesser extent, Malkuth. They symbolise our intention of setting out on our chosen spiritual path. The sandals are worn only within the temple.

The Girdle

The girdle is the traditional garment of Venus, and hence, Netzach. It symbolises the binding obligation of initiation and the self-imposed controls placed upon us by the discipline of magic.

The Holy Oil

Various types of holy oil are used in ritual. They have similar effects to incense in that they provide a means of transmitting various forces. The holy oil is usually used for anointing purposes. Anointing as a religious or magical ritual has a long and distinguished history, in fact most ceremonial coronation and ordination rituals include the process of anointing even today. The ancient Egyptians, Greeks and Romans lay great stress upon anointing and frequent references to it may be found in the bible.

Anointing can be a very potent ritual act, especially when it is desired to transfer or confer power, and as such it should be used rather more frequently within the magical lodge or temple than has recently been the custom. The best anointing oils are strong, pure and possessed of an inner warmth, which is difficult, if not impossible, to describe to one who has never experienced their application. The holy oil is usually attributed to Tiphareth and elementally to fire. One of the most famous holy oils of all time is that disclosed in the *"Book of the Sacred Magic of Abramelin the Mage"*, a fifteenth century discourse on high magic translated by S. L. MacGregor-Mathers, co-founder of the Golden Dawn in the nineteenth century. The holy oil of Abramelin consists of myrrh, galangal, cinnamon and olive oil formed into a fragrant, golden balsam. It is certainly a powerful and evocative perfume. The holy oil is stored within a crystal vial with a silver stopper within the magician's altar. It should not be exposed to light or kept within a common glass or plastic container.

The Outer Robe of Concealment

This most important article of ritual clothing is attributed to Binah and the shroud of form around the inner life principle. It is closely related to the sea of darkness, which is also Binah. For this reason the outer robe in practice is usually black and unadorned by decorations or symbols of any kind.

The Inner Robe of Glory

As the outer robe of darkness is attributed to Binah, the Mother, so is the inner robe of light attributed to Chokmah, the Father, for it represents the dynamic energy of life contained within the veil of matter. The inner robe of glory is the life spirit of the magician, the vital spark that burns within, and it is symbolically embossed with symbols expressing his total dedication to the Great Work. Force contained by form, and form ensouled by force are personified by the symbolic inner robe of the magician. In practice, the inner robe is white, with any symbols applied in gold, for these two colours best typify the pure and noble intentions behind the apparently dark and mysterious apparel of high magic.

The Pillars

Only the most fortunate of modern practitioners will be able to erect a pair of temple pillars, most would count themselves very lucky to have a cupboard that can be converted to a temple! The restrictions of modern living conditions effectively prohibit most of us ever constructing a full scale temple complete with chequered floor and symbolic furniture.

The black pillar of severity is headed by Binah, and the white pillar of mercy is likewise headed by Chokmah. The essence of the pillars is polarity, pure and simple.

The function of the pillars within the temple is to provide two extremes which must be balanced if we are to pass between them. The pillars frequently serve as a gateway to other dimensions, a trigger to the subconsciousness denoting the crossing of the bridge between Malkuth and Yesod. When the magician dons his sandals and passes between the pillars he expects to go places!

Pillar construction can be a demanding and expensive process, beyond all but the most wealthy and fortunate, but thankfully it is also possible to make a first class pair of ritual pillars which are both portable, cheap and which do not require any special facilities.

The answer may well be found at your local carpet store where the rolls which modern carpets are wrapped around provide a perfectly round, heavy duty cardboard tube ideally suited to painting black or white. These should be cut to length and mounted upon a square wooden base for stability.

The Elemental Lamps

These are by no means common items of ritual hardware, but they are certainly one of the most effective. They consist of four small night-light candles behind suitably coloured glass windows cut in an outer container of metal. Their construction is extremely simple, but their effect in the temple is profound. The cut-outs that form the windows should be in the design of the kerubic figures of Leo, Scorpio, Taurus and Aquarius. The backing glasses should be red, blue, green and yellow respectively, representing fire, water, earth and air. The elemental lamps are ruled by Auriel and are attributed to Malkuth.

Having discussed the theory behind our primary weapons, and examined the function of some of the secondary artefacts of ritual, it is now time to begin our practical work – the actual making and consecration of our personal set of ceremonial regalia.

7 MAKING THE WEAPONS

The physical act of gathering the materials and necessary tools, preparing the work-place, carefully following the instructions and making the weapons themselves is, in itself, a kind of ritual. Even cleaning and tidying up afterwards can have inner meaning, akin to 'closing the circle'. It is worth noting that the often demanding requirements expressed in ancient grimoires and spell-books, such as the gathering of herbs by the light of a full moon, or by seeking out hard-to-acquire ingredients, all served a real purpose. They were, in some senses, a kind of 'quest', the accomplishment of which served to concentrate and focus the mind, and most critically, the Will of the operator. There is, therefore, quite a difference between buying magical items ready-made from a store as opposed to investing some of yourself in them by being involved in their creation. Thankfully, these days we have no need of the wing of a bat, or the tongue of a lizard, though a powered multi-tool might come in useful! All of the designs that follow are relatively easy to make, and once constructed, will give good service for many years. It will prove to be well worth the effort.

The Water Chalice

The Water Chalice

Materials

One silver-plated chalice
One piece of silver sheet 50mm x 25mm
Blue cold enamel resin

Construction

Unless the magician also happens to be a highly skilled silversmith with access to a fully equipped workshop, there is no way in which he can hope to produce an acceptable chalice 'from scratch' as it were. This leaves but one viable alternative, and that is to decorate an existing chalice. This may be accomplished in several ways, from applying coloured paper to it with glue (as advocated in the Golden Dawn) to attempting to paint the required designs upon it. Neither is very satisfactory, either in appearance or durability. The answer to the magician's prayers has, however, manifested in the form of substances known as cold enamels. These are based upon epoxy resins and, when set, are virtually impossible to distinguish from their traditional glass counterparts. The main advantage is that no heat is required at any time during the enamelling process; hence, they may be applied to plated objects which would be destroyed by the normal enamelling procedure. This makes enamelling by otherwise unskilled persons a practical reality, and only a few experiments will testify to the excellent effects which may be obtained. Various colours are available, and different grades set within different time limits, so it is vital that the particular manufacturer's instructions are followed to the letter. These are usually included with the enamels at the time of purchase. Follow the instructions here in the order they are listed:

1. Two different designs are to be overlaid upon the chalice - the kerubic sign of water, the eagle head, and the equal-armed cross of the elements. Each is applied twice, making four overlaid designs in all. These are drawn full size (see on the next page) for you to copy. These copies then serve as templates. Stick these templates to the surface of the sheet silver with contact adhesive then cut out the centre designs with a piercing saw. Use the supporting jig shown below to rest the work upon while cutting.

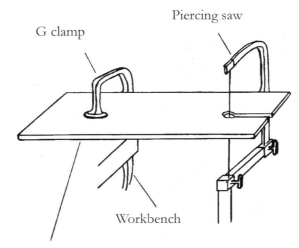

2. After cutting the centre designs out, cut out the outer circles. For cutting internal shapes drill a small hole to permit access by the saw blade. After cutting out the designs, clean up any rough edges with a fine file.

Equal-armed cross   **Kerubic sign of Water**

3. Mix a small quantity of transparent epoxy resin and coat the back of the design to be overlaid. Carefully position this on the chalice. Remember to lay the chalice on its side during this stage of the operation to lessen the likelihood of the overlay slipping. Wipe off any excess adhesive with surgical cotton-tipped sticks dipped in methylated spirit. It may be necessary to bend the overlays to conform to the curve of the chalice walls; if this is so, then it will help to apply gentle pressure to the overlay whilst the adhesive sets to prevent it springing back to its previous shape. The best way of achieving this is to use strong elastic bands strategically placed around the bowl of the chalice. Leave these in position until the adhesive has firmly set.

4. Mix the cold enamel in accordance with the manufacturer's instructions. Apply it to the cut out in the centre of the overlay with a fine spatula or cheap artist's brush. Do not waste an expensive brush on this task for the enamel will quickly ruin it. Remove any excess with the recommended solvent.

5. Allow each overlay to set firmly before moving on to the next. This may take up to 24 hours, depending on the particular make of enamel you are using. Rushing at this stage will cause runs and the possibility of permanent damage.

6. After each of the overlays has been filled with the enamel examine them for any small splashes or overlapping areas of enamel. These can be sanded flush with the finest 'wet and dry' paper as used on auto paint finishes. Take very great care not to scratch the surrounding silver.

7. To finish, give a good buff with non-scratch silver polish.

8. The appropriate god-names must now be added to the chalice (see Appendix). This is a job for a professional engraver for one slip would ruin everything. You may be lucky and find an engraver who is able to engrave in Hebrew, but this is unlikely. Most of us will have to use the English equivalents of Hebrew letters. In the case of the water chalice these would be Gabriel, the archangel, and El, the god-name. It is best to have this done at the time you purchase the chalice and to add the overlays afterwards.

9. The completed chalice should be wrapped in a blue silk cover to await consecration.

THE AIR WAND

Many different designs of wand are encountered. A major factor in design being the elemental or other attribution involved. If you attribute your wand to fire, for instance, your design will be considerably altered from that of another magician using an air attribution. To complicate matters further, many magicians use several wands - each formulated to correspond with a particular aspect of force, generally a planetary or sephirothic attribution is intended, but on occasions other symbols may be employed.

The simplest form of wand is the 'Rod of Power', which most magicians possess even if they own a whole battery of other, more specialised wands. This rod of power represents the 'inner will' of the individual magician and is held in special regard. It usually consists of no more than a rod of hazel or almond wood, possibly tipped with iron, silver or copper, and on rare occasions with a precious stone such as a star sapphire. It should be noted that this rod of power is not an elemental weapon but is attributed to the principle of spirit and sephirah Kether in particular. The rod of power, once made, is usually kept hidden from profane eyes and is periodically anointed with the holy oil of Abramelin. It is kept wrapped in a pure white cover of natural silk.

Other wands are encountered, some of which go by rather grand sounding titles like 'Chief Adept's Wand', 'Lotus Wand' and the 'Hierophant's Wand'. These are derived from the Order of the Golden Dawn rituals and details of their design will be found in Israel Regardie's fine book *"The Golden Dawn"*. Construction of these should pose no problem as the techniques given here are quite adaptable.

The wand described in detail is essentially a hermetic caduceus wand with particular relevance to sephirah Hod and, to a lesser extent, sephirah Chesed. It is also very much a 'Middle Pillar" weapon and therefore well suited to general ceremonial use.

As wand design is a personal thing, you are advised to take the ideas and techniques given here and adapt them to your own personal ideal.

Materials

A turned piece of ebony or other hardwood 560mm in length by 17mm in diameter. Wood intended for making flutes is often the most suitable.
25mm X 25mm hardwood square
50mm diameter hardwood ball
50mm square of medium gauge brass sheet
One 75mm length of 4mm diameter brass rod
Assorted paints

Construction

1. Drill a hole of equivalent size to the rod in the hardwood ball. Check that this makes a tight fit. To ensure accuracy and avoid splitting, drill a pilot hole of smaller diameter first. Be careful not to drill right through the ball - about half way (15mm or so) is fine.

2. Draw out the wings full size on to a piece of paper. With contact adhesive stick these onto the sheet of brass. With the jeweller's saw, cut them out. This is not at all difficult if you use the same cutting jig as described for the water chalice overlays. After cutting them out, clean up any rough edges with a fine file.

3. Drill seven 4mm holes along the side of the rod. These holes go right the way through and emerge on the opposite side. For spacings see wand construction diagram (Figure 3).

4. Drill a hole to match the diameter of the rod in the hardwood cube. Follow directions as given for the ball.

5. With enamel paint colour the ball a deep blue colour. This relates to Chesed. With olive, citrine, russet and black paint the sides of the hardwood cube. This relates to Malkuth. Alternatively, paint them with yellow, blue, red and black representing the four elements. Cold enamels may be used instead of ordinary paint and some beautiful effects can be obtained this way. Much depends upon the symbolism you prefer.

6. Cut the brass rod into six pieces approximately 60mm in length. Bend these into crescent shapes to match the holes in the side of the rod. These form the 'coils' of the serpents. To obtain a perfect match you will have to trim them to exact length with a pair of wire cutters or junior hacksaw. When all six pieces are bent to shape and fit into the corresponding holes on the side of the rod with case, coat the ends with epoxy cement and glue them into position.

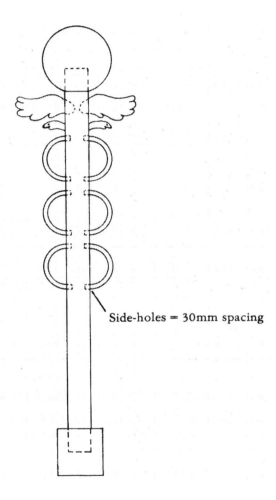

Side-holes = 30mm spacing

7. Drill two more holes just above the uppermost 'coil' of the serpent and fix two more pieces of brass rod into place to serve as the heads of the serpents. The shape of the 'head' can be formed of plastic wood or modelling compound and then painted.

8. Above these drill two more holes and glue the brass wings into place. The wings may require supporting with adhesive tape until the glue sets.

9. Coat both ends of the rod with epoxy cement and glue both the ball and the cube to the rod. Allow to set hard before disturbing.

10. With a sharp modelling knife and sandpaper clean off any glue 'squeeze' and then polish all metal parts with brass cleaning and polishing solution.

11. With a fine lining brush paint the Hebrew names (see p. 168) upon the side of the rod. Allow to dry well before giving a final sealing coat of polyurethane varnish to protect against handling.

12. The completed wand may be wrapped in a yellow silk cover to await consecration.

The above directions can easily be adapted to produce other designs if required. The ball can be replaced with a triple flame signifying the Hebrew letter 'Shin' or even by elaborate carved heads of the Egyptian god-forms.

Making the Weapons

The Wand or Rod

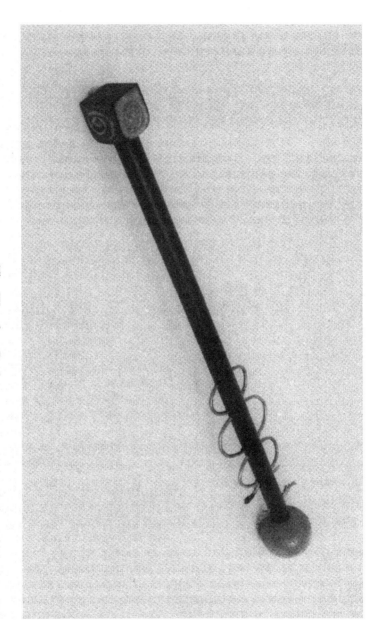

THE SWORD

Materials

Two pieces suitable hardwood approx 160mm X 40mm X 10mm
A suitable sword as a basis for modification
A sheet of silver approx 50mm X 20mm X 1mm to 1.5mm thick

Construction

The comments made in regard to manufacture from scratch of the water chalice apply equally to the mighty sword of power. Unless the magician is a qualified metal worker, with a good workshop available, the prospect of producing a workmanlike sword is rather slender. For this reason it is suggested that a ready-made sword be obtained from an occult or masonic supply house and 'customised' by the addition of a specially modified hilt carrying the appropriate archangelic names and sigils etc. Good swords at reasonable prices may also be obtained through shops dealing with imported goods from the far east, and admirable ritual swords can be fashioned using these as a base. When choosing a sword for modification examine the hilt carefully in the light of the instructions that follow, as a very few may prove impossible to modify in the manner described. Most, however, will cause no problems.

1. Depending upon the exact size and design of the existing sword hilt trim the two pieces of ebony or other hardwood to approximate shape.

2. With a metal file prepare two flat areas on the side faces of the hilt to receive the overlaid ebony pieces.

3. Carefully trim the ebony pieces to match exactly the flat areas on the hilt. With a medium wood rasp and coarse sandpaper contour them until they provide a comfortable grip. Test this by gripping them whilst held in position against the hilt.

4. With a fine grit sandpaper remove any rasp marks and smooth the ebony pieces to a fine finish.

5. Copy the archangelic name of Khamael in Hebrew letters (see p. 169) onto paper. Stick the letters individually onto the sheet of silver; use contact adhesive for this, never under any circumstances use epoxy.

6. Using the cutting jig shown previously (figure 1) and a piercing saw fitted with a fine blade, carefully cut out each letter in turn.

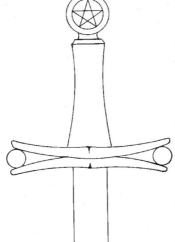

7. After cutting out the letters of the name, file them to a perfect finish with miniature files. Those used by watch repairers are ideal for this task.

8. At this point also prepare in a similar manner any other sigils, names or designs you wish to add to the sword. As the sword is principally a weapon of Geburah, the god-name of the sephirah, *Elohim Gibor* is frequently chosen.

This will be inlaid on the opposite side of the hilt to the archangelic name.

9. To begin the inlaying process, lay out the letters upon the ebony overlay and check for positioning. When satisfied, take each letter in turn and apply a very small quantity of contact adhesive to it. Stick it lightly in position. When all are positioned in this manner, let the adhesive set for a few minutes.

10. It is now necessary to mark the exact outlines of each letter upon the wood of the hilt overlay. This can be done in several ways, including scribing around them, but this tends to disturb the positioning of the pieces and can result in errors. A better way is to paint the surrounding area with a coat of enamel paint of contrasting colour; for ebony, yellow is best. This is applied all around the letters, leaving an outline like a stencil in reverse when the letters are removed after the paint has dried. A fine scalpel or razor blade is best employed to remove the fragile letters without damage.

11. It is at this stage where most mistakes occur, for it is now necessary to carefully rout out the outlines of the letters in the wood of the overlay. The best tool for this job is a Dremel or similar multi-tool fitted with 'dental burr' type routing bits. This accomplishes the task in next to no time with astonishing ease and accuracy. The small rotary drills used by model enthusiasts will also accept miniature routing bits and can yield similar excellent results. If you do not have access to any power tools then you will have to use model making knives and gouges and do the best you can by hand. But, if at all possible, try and use power tools; the time factor and the excellence of results gained by the use of them make it well worthwhile seeking them out.

12. After the routing has been accomplished, check the evenness of depth by laying the letters in the hollowed out compartments that

The Sword

you have already prepared. If they are seated too low (that is, below the surface) they will be invisible when the filler is applied, so if this is the case, mix some epoxy resin and refill the routed section until the correct height is achieved.

13. When the routed sections are perfectly prepared, mix a small quantity of black cold enamel, or some epoxy resin stained black with dye-stuff, and lay this in the letter channels. Quickly place each letter in turn into its allocated place, squeezing out a small quantity of epoxy as it is pressed into position. Allow to set.

14. With coarse grade sandpaper, remove any excess filler and flush the letters down to the surface. Any pin-holes not filled with resin may now be refilled.

15. To finish the inlaying give a final smooth over with fine grit 'wet and dry' paper. The filler should be more or less invisible. If you have used another wood instead of ebony you must tint the filler so that it matches the particular wood used as closely as possible. Furniture maker's supply houses sell powdered 'earth colours' for this purpose, but powdered art paints work just as well.

16. When the inlaying has been completed to your satisfaction, fix the wood hilt overlays to the sword proper by coating both surfaces with epoxy cement and clamping each overlay to the hilt of the sword in turn. Any excess glue 'squeeze' can be removed before setting with a rag lightly soaked in solvent. Allow it all to set for several hours before handling.

17. The completed sword hilt should be given a good polish with a wax furniture polish.

THE FIRE DAGGER

Materials

A stiletto carbon steel dagger blade approx 160mm long
Silver fittings off an antique knife
A piece of ebony or other fine quality hardwood approx 95mm X 20mm X 10mm in size for the hilt
Enamel paint or brass or silver sheet to inlay divine names

Construction

    Since forging an acceptable knife blade from iron ore is beyond the facilities and capabilities of most people (the present author included), it was decided to utilise one of the excellent ready-made dagger blades which are available from most occult supply firms. These blades are of first class quality and are highly recommended. The only task then required is to make a suitable handle to match. I was fortunate in that I had a set of solid silver dagger fittings already available that I had previously removed from an antique knife with a less than satisfactory blade. This set of fittings was then used in conjunction with a freshly purchased blade and handmade ebony handle to produce my fire dagger. A good source of silver fittings are the highly decorated Victorian table knives seen in antique dealer's or auction rooms. An 'odd' knife can be purchased at very reasonable cost, and dismantled to provide fittings of far higher quality than would otherwise be available.

    For a black-handled knife, ebony is by far the best wood, but as it is not easy to come by these days you can use boxwood, sycamore or holly stained black to give a similar effect. For a white-handled knife, unstained holly or boxwood is recommended. On no account use a softwood.

1. Draw the required outline of the dagger handle on to the piece of wood. Cut this out with a bandsaw or a coping saw.

2. With a medium-coarse wood rasp, roughly shape it, taking care not to work against the grain as this can cause splits. The contours should be gentle to enable comfortable handling.

3. When shaped with the wood rasp, graduate to sanding with first coarse, then fine grits of sandpaper.

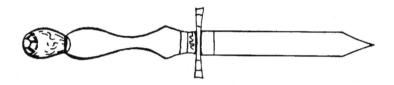

4. The tang on most blades is far too long, so with a hacksaw reduce this to approximately 50mm long. Then clamp the semi-finished wooden handle in a vice, or other stable holder, and with a fine drill make a pilot hole lengthwise down the handle. With gradually increasing drill sizes enlarge this to receive the tang of the blade. Be careful not to force the drill, and especially careful to maintain a central position; both spell disaster if not accomplished correctly.

5. Trim the wooden handle so that it will receive the fittings. This is done with sandpaper and a small file. Place the cross guard on the blade, coat the tang with epoxy resin, and force some into handle. Carefully thread the handle onto the tang; pay particular attention to keeping the handle straight, and avoiding any twisting. Once set, the only way to remove the handle if an error has been made is to break the wood of the handle away piece by piece.

6. When fully set, remove any excess epoxy resin with a sharp blade and sandpaper. Any large overflows are best removed when the adhesive is partly set, when it is still elastic and can easily be scraped off. If handling the knife in this state be especially careful not to disturb the positioning of the handle.

7. Depending on the type of pommel you are using, you should shape the end of the wooden handle to receive this and coat both surfaces with epoxy cement. Bring together, making sure of positioning, and allow to set hard before handling.

8. Finish the handle by polishing the ebony with wire wool and linseed oil for a perfect, satin smooth surface. The silver parts should be given a final bluff with a soft rag and metal polish.

9. Add the name of the archangelic intelligence of fire, Michael, in enamel paint or, if preferred, in brass or silver letters inlaid into the handle. For details of this technique see the sword section. Hebrew letters should be used for best effect (see p. 168).

10. A Calvary Cross, symbol of Tiphareth, may also be inlaid into the handle if desired. Either brass or silver may be used with good effect.

The Symbolic Weapons of Ritual Magic

The Fire Dagger

Making the Weapons

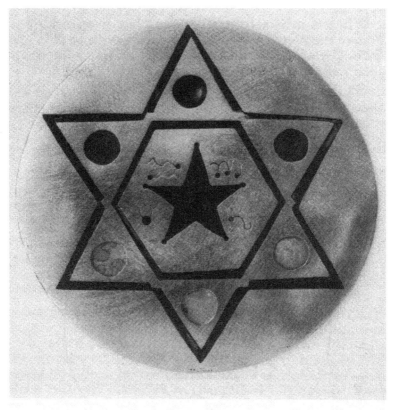

Pantacle

THE PANTACLE

Materials

Two 100mm diameter discs of medium gauge sheet brass
Set of cold enamels in red, orange, green, blue, black and violet

Construction

1. Mark out the design of the pantacle onto one of the brass discs. This may be drawn on with a graver, or more simply, drawn onto paper and glued on with contact adhesive to act as a guide.

2. With a fine piercing saw cut out the central hexagon. To gain blade access you will have to drill small holes to thread the blade through. After threading the blade into the hole, adjust the saw tension once more to allow cutting. One small hole at each corner not only permits easy access, but also makes negotiating the angles far easier.

3. With a medium file, clean up any rough edges, both on the hexagon and inside of the marked out hexagram.

4. Drill more holes around the outside of the hexagram. Using the same techniques as above, cut it out with the piercing saw. With a medium file, finish off the edges so that no uneven or jagged metal remains. Check the fit of the hexagon and hexagram within the disc. If the edges seem unbalanced clean them up with a file.

5. In the centre of each of the 'points' of the hexagram, drill a 9mm hole. To avoid inaccuracy, drill a small pilot hole first. Clean up any rough edges with a round 'rat tail' file.

6 . Using the 'hole and threaded blade' technique, cut out the central pentagram. With a small triangular file clean up any rough edges.

7. When all the various sections have been cut from the disc, check for irregularities and misalignment. Small errors may be corrected by judicious application of a file. For an accurate check, place the pieces on a second brass disc which serves as a backing.

8. When a satisfactory alignment has been achieved, remove the pieces and coat with epoxy resin to glue into place. Use a slow setting glue to permit fine adjustment when the surfaces are brought together.

9. When the pieces are glued into position, and the adhesive has set hard, clean up the edges of the two discs to a perfect finish.

10. Mix the various colours of cold enamel in accordance with the manufacturer's instructions. Small tinfoil cake containers are ideal for this purpose. The 9mm holes in the hexagram points are filled first, in the following colours:

Top point black: SUPERNAL TRIAD
Top right point blue: CHESED

Top left point red: GEBURAH
Lower right point green: NETZACH
Lower left point orange: HOD
Lowest point violet: YESOD

The central pentagram is filled with deep mauve resin at the same time as the sephirothic points are filled.

11. When the sephirothic colours have set hard, fill the gaps around the hexagon and hexagram with black resin. It does not matter if any overspill occurs as this can easily be sanded off when dry. Likewise, any 'dents' or other gaps can easily be filled later with more resin.

12. When the black resin has set hard (leave for several days) the entire pantacle should be sanded with wet and dry paper to provide a perfect finish. A final gloss is given with brass polish.

13. Divine names can be painted around the pantacle with enamel paint or added to the reverse. The kerubic signs of the elements may also be placed around the central pentagram if desired.

Caution: Drilling holes of large diameter in metal can be dangerous unless the workpiece is firmly secured, especially if power tools are used. The drill can 'snatch' or grab at the workpiece causing it to rotate at high speed with possibly serious consequences. Make sure that the workpiece is firmly clamped so that this is impossible. Keep the hands and fingers well away from the workpiece whilst drilling is in progress. Always wear eye protection when filing or working metal by machine.

8 RITUAL CONSECRATION OF THE MAGICAL WEAPONS

Before the weapons may be employed in magical ritual they must first be banished and then dedicated by an act of ceremonial consecration. The banishing rites will remove all traces of undesirable or irrelevant forces from the aura of the weapons, and the consecration rites cause an influx of the specific forces required by the magician. A good illustration of this principle may be found by examining a piece of magnetic recording media. If the tape contains existing recordings, any attempt to place a second recording on top is useless, unless we first erase the existing track. Failure to do so results in a chaotic jumble of conflicting speech, music or data, and should the magician fail to erase the psychic influences present in the raw materials of his weapons he will in all probability experience similar effects. It is therefore vital that proper banishing and consecration rituals are performed on all weapons intended for use in ceremonial magic.

The consecration rites given here are based upon the Enochian system of magic received originally by Dr John Dee and Edward Kelley in the late sixteenth century and expanded upon considerably by the Hermetic Order of the Golden Dawn in the latter half of the nineteenth century. To obtain a full comprehension of the Enochian system takes many years of intensive study, and many of its mysteries are still concealed after decades of diligent research by students of the occult. However, enough is known of the system to work it effectively, and the results obtained tend to support the view held by many magicians that it is possibly one of the most direct and powerful systems of ritual magic in existence.

Since this book was first published in 1983, quite a lot more has been learned about the origins and translation of Enochian. However, rather than change and update the rituals as originally presented, they are here preserved intact as they are a good reflection of how Enochian was actually used in the early 1980's, but by all means feel free to modify or update them if you feel it to be necessary. Be assured that exactly as presented below, these rituals are highly effective.

In view of the above comments, the student is recommended to study the main source books on the Enochian system before attempting the rituals described below. A list of these will be found in the bibliography. To plunge headlong into Enochian with little or no comprehension of the forces involved is certainly not recommended. It is also the case that many alternative forms of consecration rituals exist, and are equally effective if performed with the required commitment and intent.

Such extended rituals may seem archaic, verbose and ponderous to some. However, there are good reasons why this is so, although the reasons are not necessarily at all obvious. This is a subject to be addressed elsewhere, suffice to say that as in many things, you rarely receive much, if anything, of value unless you first invest sufficient effort in it, and that magic is no different. Ritual performed without the 'inner circuits' being properly made and correctly 'tuned in' is an empty vessel. When the circuits are correct, however, and a full strength signal is being received, it is something else altogether.

The rituals described are complete in themselves, and if performed as directed, with correct visualisations and name vibrations, will cause the newly-made weapons to become active at inner levels far beyond the normal elemental regions. Weapons consecrated in this manner will be extremely potent in the right hands, and should be treated as sacred thereafter. For by these rituals divinity does indeed descend.

Consecration of the Water Chalice

Let the temple be provided with an altar set with holy water, incense burner and incense formulated to be favourable to the element of water, a container of salt, the implement to be consecrated and a lamp of holy oil or a candle. Let the four Enochian tablets be positioned to the quarters, and let the tablet of union lie upon the altar, which should be situated in the centre of the circle.

1. Perform the Lesser Banishing Ritual of the Pentagram.

2. Perform the Lesser Banishing Ritual of the Hexagram.

3. Take up the Holy water and circumambulate deosil saying:
"So therefore first the priest who governeth the works of fire must sprinkle with the lustral water of the loud resounding sea"

4. Take up the censer and circumambulate deosil saying:
"And when, after all the phantoms are vanished, thou shalt see that Holy formless fire, that fire which darts and flashes

through the hidden depths of the Universe. Hear thou the voice of fire".

Cense each quarter in the sign of a cross as you reach it, and pause for a moment at each. Visualise the fire as it cleanses the aura.

5. Circumambulate deosil thrice, saying:
"Holy art thou, Lord of the Universe, Holy art thou, whom nature hath not formed Holy art thou, the vast and mighty one, Lord of the Light and of the Darkness"

6. Perform the Greater Invoking Ritual of the Pentagram of Water.

7. Stand by the altar facing west. Make the invoking pentagram of water over the chalice. Begin the following invocation:
"Thou who art everlasting, thou who has created all things, and doth clothe thyself with the forces of nature as with a garment, by thy Holy and Divine Name El, I beseech thee to grant unto me strength and insight for my search after the Hidden Light and the Waters of remembrance and Wisdom. I entreat thee to cause thy wonderful Archangel Gabriel, bearer of the mystic horn, who poureth the waters of life to the firmaments of the earth to guide me in this path and furthermore to direct thine Angel Taliahad to guide my steps therein. May the powerful Prince Tharsis, by the gracious permission of the infinite supreme, be present here now, and bestow upon this Holy Chalice the power to govern all that pertains to the nature of water"

8. Make the invoking pentagram of water over the chalice, and say:
"And Elohim said, let us make Adam in our own image, after our likeness, and let him have dominion over the fish of the sea. In the Divine and Holy names of water, and in the sign

of the Eagle, spirits of water be servient unto me, for I am a true worshipper of the Highest".

9. Visualise a blue light descend to the chalice as you intone the invocations of the holy names of God, the king of the west and the six seniors:

"In the Three Great Secret Holy Names of God borne upon the Banners of the West, Emph Arsl Gaiol, I summon Thee, thou mighty King of the West, Ra Agiosl, to attend upon this rite and by thy presence increase its effect and power. Grant that in this Holy chalice I may find a powerful weapon with which to rule with justice the spirits of the elements"

10. With the index finger trace the invoking hexagram of Saturn saying:

"Ye Mighty Princes of the Western quadrangle, I invoke you who are known to me by the honourable title and rank of Seniors. Hear my petition ye mighty princes of the Western quarter of the Earth bearing the names of Lsrahpm Sigaiol Saiinor Soniznt Laoaxrp Ligdisa and be this day present here with me that thou may bestow upon this Holy Chalice those powers of mastery over the Elements of which thou art Seniors".

11. The invocations of the angels of the lesser angles of the elemental tablets now follow:

"Oh thou powerful Angel Hnlrx, who art Lord and Ruler over the Fiery essence of the Waters, be present here now and bestow upon this Holy Chalice all those powers of which thou art Lord that by its aid I may command and instruct the

> *spirits who are servient unto thee with Wisdom and justice, for thus sayeth the Lord God of whom I am a true worshipper"*

12. Trace the invoking pentagram of water over the chalice with the kerubic sign of water, the eagle, in the centre.

13. Say:
> *"Oh thou powerful Angel Htdim, who art Lord and Ruler over the pure and fluid essences of the Waters, be present here now and bestow upon this Holy Chalice all those powers of which thou art Lord that by its aid I may command and instruct the spirits who are servient unto thee with Wisdom and justice, for thus sayeth the Lord God of whom I am a true worshipper"*

14. Trace the invoking pentagram of water over the chalice with kerubic sign as above.

15. Say:
> *"Oh thou powerful Angel Htaad, who art Lord and Ruler over the Etheric and Airy essences of the waters, be present here now and bestow upon this Holy Chalice all those powers of which thou art Lord that by its aid I may command and instruct the spirits who are servient unto thee with Wisdom and justice, for thus sayeth the Lord God of whom I am a true worshipper".*

16. Trace the invoking pentagram of water with kerubic sign as above.

17. Say:

> "Oh thou powerful Angel Hmagl, who art Lord and Ruler over the dense and solid essences of the waters, be present here now and bestow upon this Holy Chalice all those powers of which thou art Lord that by its aid I may command and instruct the spirits who are servient unto thee with Wisdom and justice, for thus sayeth the Lord God of whom I am a true worshipper".

18. Trace the invoking pentagram of water with kerubic sign as above.

19. Move to the centre of the circle standing before the chalice which lies upon the altar. Say:

> "Let us adore the Lord and King of Water. Holy art thou Lord of the Mighty Waters, Whereon thy spirit moved in the beginning, Glory be to Thee".

20. Take up the chalice and move to each of the quarters in turn and make the invoking pentagram of water at each, preceding each water pentagram with a passive invoking pentagram of spirit. Visualise the pentagrams surrounded by a blue glowing sphere, and the god-name *El* in Hebrew letters in the centre of the four water pentagrams.

21. The ritual is climaxed by the recitation of the fourth Enochian call, or key, in the original angelic language. An English translation is provided for reference:

> **"Othil lasdi babage, od dorpha, gohol: g chis ge avavago cormp pd, ds sonf viu diu? Casarmi oali mapm, sobam ag cormpo crp l, casarmg croodzi**

> *chis od ugeg; ds t, capimali, chis capimaon; od lonshin chis ta lo cla. Torgu, nor quasahi, od f caosga; bagle zir enay Iad, ds i od apila. Dooaip Qaal, zacar, od zamran obelisong, rest el aaf nor molap".*

> *"I have set my feet in the South, and have looked about me, saying: are not the thunders of increase numbered 33, which reign in the second angle? Under whom I have placed 9639, whom none has yet numbered but one, in whom the second beginning of things are and wax strong; Which also successively, are the number of time; And their powers are as the first 456. Arise, you sons of pleasure, and visit the earth for I am the Lord your God, which is and lives. In the name of the Creator, move, and show yourselves as pleasant deliverers, that you may praise him amongst the sons of men"*

22. The king of the tablet can be constrained to appear at this point. However, this is an advanced operation and best left to the discretion of the individual magician.

23. Let the magician circumambulate thrice deosil with the chalice and receive therein the influx of the cataracts of watery essence.

24. Close the temple by circumambulating thrice deosil saying:
> *"Holy art thou, Lord of the Universe, Holy art thou, whom nature hath not formed, Holy art thou, the vast and mighty one, Lord of the Light and of the Darkness".*

25. Purify the temple with water.

26. Consecrate the temple with fire.

27. Perform the Lesser Banishing Ritual of the Pentagram.

28. Perform the Lesser Banishing Ritual of the Hexagram.

29. Say:
> *"In the name of Yeheshuah I now set free any spirits imprisoned by this ceremony, depart in peace, return to your own strange abodes with the blessing of the most High of whom I am a true worshipper. I close this temple in the name of the Light supreme".*

30. Make three sharp knocks.

Notes:

1. Inexperienced practitioners should certainly omit sections 21-23, which are difficult to execute and are not, in any case, concerned with purely elemental functions. Leaving these sections out in no way lessens the effect of the ritual at elemental levels.

2. The angelic names Htaad, Htdim, Hnlrx and Hmagl are derived from the lesser angles of the water tablet, the kerubic squares, prefixed by the letter 'H' of Hcoma the 'water line' upon the tablet of union. They are archangelic in nature and force, though not so addressed in rank. They represent the operation of the sub-elements under the dominion of spirit.

3. The six seniors of the water element have planetary affiliations. These are: Lsrahpm = Mars; Slgaiol = Venus; Saiinor = Jupiter; Soaixnt = Mercury; Laoaxrp = Luna; Ligdisa = Saturn. The Elemental King, Ra Agiosl, is attributed to Sol. Ardent ritualists may wish to trace appropriate invoking hexagrams when pronouncing these names, however, this is by no means essential.

Consecration of the Air Wand

Let the temple be provided as before, with holy water, incense burner with incense favourable to the element of air, lamp and altar, etc. The four Enochian tablets should be placed in the quarters; the tablet of union to lie upon the altar.

1. Perform the Lesser Banishing Ritual of the Pentagram.

2. Perform the Lesser Banishing Ritual of the Hexagram.

3. Take up the holy water and circumambulate deosil saying:
> *"So therefore first the priest who governeth the works of fire must sprinkle with the lustral water of the loud resounding sea"*

4. Take up the censer and circumambulate deosil saying:
> *"And when, after all the phantoms are vanished, thou shalt see that holy formless fire, that fire which darts and flashes through the hidden depths of the universe. Hear thou the voice of fire".*

Cense each quarter in the sign of a cross as you reach it, and pause for a moment at each. Visualise the fire as it cleanses the aura.

5. Circumambulate deosil thrice, saying:
> *"Holy art thou, Lord of the Universe, Holy art thou, whom nature hath not formed, Holy art thou, the vast and mighty one, Lord of the Light and of the Darkness".*

6. Perform the greater invoking ritual of the pentagram of air.

7. Stand by the altar facing east. Make the invoking pentagram of air over the wand. Begin the following invocation:
> *"Thou who art everlasting, thou who has created all things, and doth clothe thyself with the forces of nature as with a garment, by thy Holy and Divine name YHVH, I beseech thee to grant unto me strength and insight for my search after the hidden light and Wisdom. I entreat thee to cause thy wonderful archangel Raphael, who governeth the works of air to guide me in this path, and furthermore to direct thine angel Chassan to guide my steps therein. May the powerful Prince Ariel, by the gracious permission of the infinite supreme be present here now, and bestow upon this Holy wand the power to govern all which pertains to the nature of air, by the power of light, Amen"*

8. Make the invoking pentagram of air over the wand. Say:
> *"And Elohim said, let us make Adam in our own image, after our likeness, and let him have dominion over the birds of the air. In the Divine and Holy names of air, and in the sign of the Head of Man, Spirits of Air be servient unto me, for I am a true worshipper of the Highest".*

9. Visualise a yellow light descend to the wand as you intone the invocations of the holy names of God, the king of the east and the six seniors:
> *"In the Three Great Secret Holy names of God, borne upon the banners of the East, Oro Ibah Aozpi I summon thee, thou great King of the East, Bataivah, to attend upon this rite and by thy presence increase its power and effect. Grant that in this Holy wand I may find a powerful weapon with which to rule with justice the spirits of the elements".*

10. With the index finger trace the invoking hexagram of Saturn saying:

> *"Ye Mighty Princes of the Eastern quadrangle, I invoke you who are known to me by the honourable title and rank of Seniors. Hear my petition, ye Mighty Princes of the Eastern quarter Of the Earth bearing the names of Habioro Ahaozpi Aaozaif Avtotar Htmorda Hipotga and be this day present here with me that thou may bestow upon this Holy wand those powers of mastery over the elements of which thou art Seniors".*

11. The invocations to the angels of the lesser angles of the elemental tablets now follow:

> *"O thou resplendent angel Exgsd, who art Lord and Ruler over the fiery essences of Air be present here now and bestow upon this Holy wand all those powers of which thou art Lord that by its aid I may command and instruct the spirits who are servient unto thee with wisdom and justice, for thus sayeth the Lord God of whom I am a true worshipper, Amen'.*

12. Trace the invoking pentagram of air over the wand with the kerubic sign of air, Aquarius, in the centre.

13. Say:

> *"O thou resplendent angel Eytpa, who art Lord and Ruler over the fluid essences of Air be present here now and bestow upon this Holy wand all those powers of which thou art Lord that by its aid I may command and instruct the spirits who are servient unto thee with wisdom and justice, for thus sayeth the Lord God of whom I am a true worshipper, Amen"*

14. Trace the invoking pentagram of air, with kerubic sign, as above.

15. Say:

> *"O thou resplendent Angel ErzIa, who art Lord and Ruler over the pure and mobile essences of air, be present here now and bestow upon this Holy wand all those powers of which thou art Lord that by its aid I may command and instruct the spirits who are servient unto thee with wisdom and justice, for thus sayeth the Lord God, of whom I am a true worshipper, Amen".*

16. Trace the invoking pentagram, with kerubic sign, as above.

17. Say:

> *"O thou resplendent angel Etnbr, who art Lord and Ruler over the denser essences of air, be present here now and bestow upon this holy wand all those powers of which thou art Lord that by its aid I may command and instruct the spirits who are servient unto thee with wisdom and justice, for thus sayeth the Lord God of whom I am a true worshipper, Amen"*

18. Trace the invoking pentagram of air, with kerubic sign, as above.

19. Move to the centre of the circle standing before the wand which lies upon the altar. Say:

> *"Let us adore the Lord and King of Air. Holy art thou Lord of the mighty skies, wherein the word was heard in the beginning. Glory be unto Thee".*

20. Take up the wand and move to each of the quarters in turn and make the invoking pentagram of air at each, preceding each air pentagram with an active invoking pentagram of spirit. Visualise the pentagrams surrounded by a yellow glowing sphere, and the God-name *YHVH* in Hebrew letters in the centre of the four air pentagrams.

21. The ritual is climaxed by the recitation of the third Enochian call, or key, in the original angelic language. An English translation is provided for reference:

> ***"Micma Goho Piad, zir comselh a zien biah os londoh. Norz chis othil gigipa, undl chis ta puim, q mospleh teloch, quiin toltorg chisi chis ge, m ozien, ds t brgda od torzul. I Ii eol balzarg, od aala thiln os netaab, dluga vomsarg lonsa capmiali vors cla, homil cocasb, fafen izizop od miinoag de g netaab, vaun nanaeel, panpir malpirgi caosg pild. Noan unalah balt od vooan. Dooiap Mad, goholor, gobus, amiran. Micma iebusoz cacacom, od dooain noar micaolz aai om; Casarmg gohia: Zacar, uniglag, od imvamar pugo plapli ananael qaan".***

> *"Behold sayeth your God, I am a circle on whose hands stand twelve kingdoms. Six are the seats of living breath, the rest are as sharp sickles, or the horns of death, wherein the creatures of the earth are and are not, except by my own hands, which shall also sleep and shall rise. In the first I made you stewards and placed you in twelve seats of government, giving unto every one of you power successively over 456, the true ages of time, to the intent that from the highest vessels the corners of your governments you might work my power, pouring down the fires of life and increase upon the earth continually. Thus you are become the skirts of justice and truth. In the name of the same*

your God, lift up, I say, yourselves. Behold his mercies flourish and his name is become mighty amongst us; in whom we say; Move, descend, and apply yourselves unto us, as unto the partakers of the secret wisdom of your Creation".

22. The Great King of the tablet may now be summoned according to a special formula.

23. Let the magician circumambulate thrice deosil with the wand and receive with it the powers of the air gathered about the circle.

24. Close the temple by circumambulating thrice deosil saying:
"Holy art thou, Lord of the Universe, Holy art thou, whom nature hath not formed, Holy art thou, the vast and mighty One, Lord of the Light and of the Darkness".

25. Purify the temple with water.

26. Consecrate the temple with fire.

27. Perform the Lesser Banishing Ritual of the Pentagram.

28. Perform the Lesser Banishing Ritual of the Hexagram.

29. Say:
"In the name of Yeheshuah I now set free any spirits imprisoned by this ceremony; depart in peace, return to your own strange abodes with the blessing of the Most High, of whom I am a true and faithful worshipper. I close this temple, and draw forth the veil in the holy names of Light supreme, Amen".

30. Strike three sharp knocks.

Notes:

1. Inexperienced practitioners should omit sections 21-23.

2. The angelic names Exgsd, Eytpa, ErzIa and Etnbr are formed of the kerubic squares of the lesser angles of the air tablet, prefixed by the letter 'E' derived from Exarp the divine name governing air on the tablet of union.

3. The six seniors have planetary affiliations as follows: Habioro = Mars; Ahaozpi = Venus; Avtotar = Mercury; Htmorda = Luna; Aaozaif = Jupiter; Hipotga = Saturn; The Elemental King, Bataivah, is related to Sol.

Consecration of the Fire Dagger

Let the altar be set as before and let the incense burner be provided with ample supplies of incense formulated to correspond to both Netzach and Tiphareth, Venus and Sol.

1. Perform the Lesser Banishing Ritual of the Pentagram.

2. Perform the Lesser Banishing Ritual of the Hexagram.

3. Take up the holy water and circumambulate deosil saying:
"So therefore first, the priest who governeth the works of fire must sprinkle with the lustral water of the loud resounding sea".

4. Take up the censer and circumambulate deosil saying:
> *"And when, after all the phantoms are vanished, thou shalt see that holy formless fire, that fire which darts and flashes through the hidden depths of the universe. Hear thou the voice of fire"*

5. Circumambulate deosil thrice saying:
> *"Holy art thou, Lord of the Universe, holy art thou, whom nature hath not formed. Holy art thou, the Vast and Mighty One, Lord of the Light and of the Darkness"*

6. Perform the Greater Invoking Ritual of the Pentagram of Fire.

7. Stand by the altar facing south. Make invoking pentagram of fire over the dagger. Begin the following invocation:
> *"Thou who art everlasting, thou who hast created all things, and doth clothe thyself with the forces of nature as with a garment, by thy Holy and Divine name Elohim. I beseech thee to grant unto me strength and insight for my search after the hidden light and wisdom. I entreat thee to cause thy wonderful archangel Michael, who governeth the works of fire to guide me in this path; and further more to direct thine angel Aral to guide my steps therein. May the powerful prince Seraph, by the gracious permission of the infinite supreme, be present here now and bestow upon this holy dagger the power to govern all which pertains to the nature of fire by the power of Light, Amen".*

8. Make invoking pentagram of fire over the dagger, say:
> *"And the Elohim moved upon the face of the waters and spake in voices of fire and there was fire, and out of the fire was shed light, and the light pierced the darkness, and the darkness was no more".*

9 . Visualise a red sphere envelope the dagger as you intone the invocations of the holy names of God, the king of the south and the six seniors:

> *"In the Three Great Secret Holy names of God, borne upon the banners of the South, Oip Teaa Pedoce, I summon thee, thou great King of the South Edelprna to attend upon this rite and by thy presence increase its power and effect. Grant that in this Holy dagger I may find a powerful weapon with which to rule with justice the spirits of the elements".*

10. With the index finger trace the invoking hexagram of Saturn saying:

> *"Ye Mighty Princes of the Southern quadrangle, I invoke you who are known to me by the honourable title and rank of Seniors. Hear my petition, ye Mighty Princes of the Southern quarter of the earth bearing the names of Aaetpoi Aapdoce Adoeoet Anodoin Alndvod Arinnap, and be this day present here with me that thou may bestow upon this Holy dagger those powers of mastery over the elements of which thou art Seniors"*

11. The invocations to the angels of the lesser angles of the elemental tablet now follow:

> *"O thou mighty angel Bziza, who art Lord and Ruler over the very essence of fire, be present here now and bestow upon this Holy dagger all those powers of which thou art Lord that by its aid I may command and instruct the spirits who are servient unto thee with wisdom and justice, for thus sayeth the Lord God of whom I am a true worshipper, Amen".*

12. Trace the invoking pentagram of fire over the dagger with the kerubic sign of fire, Leo, in the centre.

13. Say:

"O thou mighty Angel Banaa, who art Lord and Ruler over the fluid essence of fire, be present here now and bestow upon this Holy dagger all those powers of which thou art Lord that by its aid I may command and instruct the spirits who are servient unto thee with wisdom and justice, for thus sayeth the Lord God of whom I am a true worshipper, Amen".

14. Trace the invoking pentagram of fire over the dagger with the kerubic sign of fire, Leo, in the centre.

15. Say:

"O thou mighty angel Bdopa, who art Lord and Ruler over the Air essences of fire be present here now and bestow upon this Holy dagger all those powers of which thou art Lord that by its aid I may command and instruct the spirits who are servient unto thee with wisdom and justice, for thus sayeth the Lord God of whom I am a true worshipper, Amen".

16. Trace the invoking pentagram of fire over the dagger with the kerubic sign of fire, Leo, in the centre.

17. Say:

"Oh thou mighty angel Bpsac, who art Lord and Ruler over the denser aspects of the fiery essence, be present here now and bestow upon this Holy dagger all those powers of which thou art Lord that by its aid I may command and instruct the spirits who are servient to thee with wisdom and justice, for thus sayeth the Lord God of whom I am a true worshipper, Amen".

18. Trace the invoking pentagram of fire with kerubic sign as above.

19. Move to the centre of the circle standing before the dagger which lies on the altar. Say:

> *"Let us adore the Lord and King of Fire. In the divine names IHVH SABAOTH and IHVH ALOAH Va DAAT spirits of fire, flames of the lamp, harsh tongues of iron, hear thou the voice of fire and adore thy creator. O mighty and unassailable one, Lord of the Light and of the Darkness, we burn with eternal aspirations unto thee! As the Elohim thou moved upon the face of the waters and spake in voices of fire male and female, bud and leaf, seed and fruit and didst create them all. Spirits of fire hear now the voice of fire".*

20. Take up the dagger and move to each of the quarters in turn and make the invoking pentagram of fire, preceding each fire pentagram with an active invoking pentagram of spirit. Visualise the pentagrams surrounded by a bright red glowing sphere and the god-name Elohim in Hebrew letters in the centre of each pentagram of Fire.

21. The ritual is climaxed by the recitation of the sixth Enochian call in the original angelic language. An English translation is provided for reference:

> **"Gab s diu em, micalzo pilzin sobam el harg mir babalon odobloc samvelg, dlugar malprg ar caosgi, od acam canal; sobol zar f bliard caosgi, od chis a netab od miam ta viu od d. Darsar solpeth bien brita od zacam g micalzo sobba ath trian luiabe od ecrin Mad qaaon".**

> *"The spirits of the fourth angle are nine, mighty in the firmament of the waters whom the first has planted as a torment to the wicked and a garland to the righteous, giving unto them fiery darts to cripple the earth, and 7699 continual workmen whose courses visit with comfort the earth, and are in government and continuance as the second and third. Wherefore hearken unto my voice. I have talked of you and I move you in power and presence you whose works shall be a song of honour and the praise of your God in your creation".*

22. The great king of the tablet may be summoned according to a special formula.

23. Let the magician circumambulate the circle thrice deosil with the dagger gathering unto it those fiery essences gathered without.

24. Close the temple by circumambulating thrice deosil saying:
> *"Holy art thou, Lord of the Universe, Holy art thou, whom nature hath not formed, Holy art thou, the vast and mighty One, Lord of the Light and of the Darkness".*

25. Purify the temple with water.

26. Consecrate the temple with fire.

27. Perform the Lesser Banishing Ritual of the Pentagram.

28. Perform the Lesser Banishing Ritual of the Hexagram.

29. Say:

> *"In the name of Yeheshua I now set free any spirits imprisoned by this ceremony, depart in peace, return to your strange abodes with the blessing of the Most High, of whom I am a true and faithful worshipper. I close this temple, and draw forth the veil in the Holy names of Light supreme, Amen"*

30. Strike three sharp knocks.

Notes:

1. Inexperienced practitioners should omit sections 21-23.

2. The angelic names Bziza, Banaa, Bdopa, and Bpsac are derived from the kerubic squares of the lesser angles of the fire tablet prefixed with the letter 'B' from Bitom, the name governing fire upon the tablet of union.

3. The six seniors have planetary attributions as follows: Aatpoi = Mars; Aapdoce = Venus; Adoeoet = Jupiter; Anodoin = Mercury; Alndvod = Luna; Arinnap = Saturn; The elemental king, Edelprna, is attributed to Sol.

Consecration of the Earth Pantacle

Let the altar be set as before and let the incense burner be provided with ample supplies of heavy, earthy incense formulated to correspond with both Kether and Malkuth. This incense shall encompass all things from the densest portion of creation to zero. It shall encompass ingredients correlating to all twelve signs of the zodiac.

1. Perform the Lesser Banishing Ritual of the Pentagram.

2. Perform the Lesser Banishing Ritual of the Hexagram.

3. Take up the Holy water and circumambulate deosil saying:
"So therefore first the priest who governeth the works of fire must sprinkle with the lustral water of the loud resounding sea".

4. Take up the censer and circumambulate deosil saying:
"And when all the phantoms are vanished thou shalt see that Holy formless fire, that fire which darts and flashes through the hidden depths of the universe. Hear thou the voice of fire".

5. Circumambulate thrice deosil saying:
"Holy art thou, Lord of the Universe, Holy art thou, whom nature hath not formed, Holy art thou, the vast and mighty One, Lord of the Light and of the Darkness"

6. Perform the Greater Invoking Ritual of the Pentagram of Earth.

7. Stand by the altar facing north. Make invoking pentagram of Earth over the pantacle. Begin the following invocation:

"Thou who art everlasting, thou who has created all things, and doth clothe thyself with the forces of nature as with a garment, by the Holy and Divine name Adonai I beseech thee to grant unto me strength and insight for my search after the hidden light and wisdom. I entreat thee to cause thy wonderful archangel Auriel who governeth the works of earth, to guide me in this path; and furthermore to direct thine angel Phorlakh to guide my steps therein. May the powerful prince kerub by the gracious permission of the infinite supreme be present here now and bestow upon this holy pantacle the power to govern all which pertains to the nature of Earth"

8. Make the Invoking pentagram of Earth over the pantacle. Say:
"And the Elohim said, let us make Adam in our own image, after our likeness, and let him have dominion over the cattle and all over the earth, and over every creeping thing that creepeth over the earth"

9. Visualise a brown-black sphere envelope the pantacle as you intone the invocations of the holy names of God, the king of the north and the six seniors:
"In the Three Great Secret Holy names of God, borne upon the banners of the North, Mor Dial Hctga, I summon thee, thou great King of the North, Iczhhcal, to attend upon this rite and by thy presence increase its power and effect. Grant that in this Holy pantacle I may find a powerful weapon and an invincible defence and that by its aid I may rule with justice the spirits of the elements"

10. With the index finger trace the invoking hexagram of Saturn saying:

> "Ye mighty princes of the Northern quadrangle, I invoke you who are known to me by the honourable title and rank of Seniors. Hear my petition ye mighty Princes of the Northern quarter of the Earth and be present here now"

11. Touch each triangle of the hexagram drawn upon the pantacle in turn as you vibrate the names of the seniors in this order:

Top point: Black - *'Liiansa'*
Right top point: Blue - *'Aczinor'*
Right lowest point: Green - *'Alhctga'*
Lowest point: Violet – *'Lzinopo'*
Lowest left point: Orange - *'Acmbicu'*
Left top point: Red - *'Laidrom'*

12. Say:
> *"And Jehova planted a garden in the East of Eden, and from this garden the life of man was sprung, and man was yet cast out Of that place, but a gate was left open, that by knowledge of the secret way he might pass the flaming swords and regain his place. Therefore, sayeth the Lord God of Wisdom and Knowledge, and the Divine Archangel Auriel, learn well the lessons of life and know of the planets, the stars and every concealed secret of my creation that ye might step once again within the bounds of my Holy City which is also my Garden of Light"*

13. The invocations to the angels of the lesser angles of the elemental tablet now follow:
> *"O thou glorious angel Naaom, who art Lord and Ruler over the fiery essences of Earth, be present here now and bestow upon this holy pantacle all those powers of which thou art*

Lord, that by its aid I may command and instruct the spirits who are servient unto thee with wisdom and justice, for thus sayeth the Lord God, of whom I am a true worshipper, Amen".

14. Make the Invoking pentagram of Earth with the kerubic sign of Earth, Taurus, in the centre of the pantacle.

15. Say:
"O thou glorious Angel Nphra, who art Lord and Ruler over the moist and fluid essences of Earth, be present here now and bestow upon this Holy pantacle all those powers of which thou art Lord, that by its aid I may command and instruct the spirits who are servient unto thee with wisdom and justice, for thus sayeth the Lord God, of whom I am a true worshipper, Amen".

16. Make the invoking pentagram of Earth, with kerubic sign, over the pantacle as before.

17. Say:
"O thou glorious Angel Nboza, who art Lord and Ruler over the delicate and airy essences of the Earth, be present here now and bestow upon this Holy pantacle all those powers of which thou art Lord, that by its aidI may command and instruct the spirits who are servient unto thee with wisdom and justice, for thus sayeth the Lord God, of whom I am a true worshipper, Amen".

18. Make invoking pentagram of Earth with kerubic sign as before.

19. Say:

> *"O thou glorious Angel Nroam, who art Lord and Ruler over the dense and solid essences of Earth, be present here now and bestow upon this Holy pantacle all those powers of which thou art Lord, that by its aid I may command and instruct the spirits who are servient unto thee with wisdom and justice, for thus sayeth the Lord God, of whom I am a true worshipper, Amen".*

20. Make the invoking pentagram of Earth, with kerubic sign, as before.

21. Move to the centre of the circle and standing before the pantacle which lies upon the altar say:

> *"Let us adore the Lord and King of Earth. Thou who created the Heavens and the Earth, the caverns of glistening stone, the mountains of shining peaks, who made the red earth and the black, and who filled the rocky seams with treasures of gold and silver, in the name of Adonai we worship thee. Let all spirits of the deep places of the earth, and of the mountain crag be servient unto thee in all the sacred and holy names which govern the firmaments of the world".*

22. Take up the pantacle and move to each of the four quarters in turn and make the invoking pentagram of Earth, preceding each Earth pentagram with a passive invoking pentagram of Spirit. Visualise the pentagrams surrounded by a dully glowing sphere of citrine, black, russet and olive with the god-name Adonai in Hebrew letters within the centre of each Earth pentagram.

23. The ritual is climaxed by the recitation of the fifth Enochian call in the original angelic language. An English translation is provided for reference.

> **"Sapah zimii d diu, od noas ta quanis Adroch dorphal caosg, od faonts piripsol ta blior casarm amipzi naz arth af, od dlugar zizop zlida caosgi tol torgi od z cbis esiasch l ta viu, od iaod thild, ds hubar peoal, soba cormfa chis ta la, uls od q cocasb. Ca niis od darbs qaas; f etbarzi od bliora iaial ednas cicles, bagle ge lad L'.**

> *"The mighty sounds have entered in the third angle and are become as olives on the Mount of Olives, looking with gladness upon the earth, and dwelling in the brightness of the Heavens as comforters unto whom I fastened pillars of gladness nineteen and gave them vessels to water the earth with all her creatures; And the are the brothers of the first and second and the beginning of their own seats, which are garnished with continual burning lamps 69636, whose numbers are as the first, the ends and the content of time. Therefore come and obey your creation; Visit us in peace and comfort; Include us as receivers of your mysteries, because our Lord and Master is all One".*

24. It is possible, at this point, to constrain the great king of the tablet to appear, but this is an advanced operation and best avoided by the novice.

25. Let the magician circumambulate thrice deosil with the pantacle and experience the powers gathered without.

26. Close the temple by circumambulating thrice deosil saying..

> *"Holy art thou, Lord of the Universe, Holy art thou, whom nature hath not formed Holy art thou, the vast and mighty One, Lord of the Light and of the Darkness".*

27. Purify the temple with water.

28. Consecrate the temple with fire.

29. Perform the Lesser Banishing Ritual of the Pentagram.

30. Perform the Lesser Banishing Ritual of the Hexagram.

31. Say:

> *"In the name of Yeheshua I now set free any spirits imprisoned by this ceremony. Depart in peace, return to your own strange abodes with the blessing of the Most High, of whom I am a true and faithful worshipper. I close this temple and draw forth the veil in the Holy name of Light supreme, Amen".*

32. Make three sharp knocks.

Notes:

1. Inexperienced practitioners should omit sections 21-25.

2. The attributions of the six seniors may be found by referring to the pantacle. The elemental king, Iczhhcal, is attributed to Sol.

3. The angelic names of the sub elements Naaom, Nphra, Nboza and Nroam are derived from the four lesser angles of the earth tablet with the addition of the letter 'N' from Nanta the line governing earth upon the tablet of union.

Ritual Consecration of the Sword of Power

1. Perform the Lesser Banishing Ritual of the Pentagram.

2. Perform the Lesser Banishing Ritual of the Hexagram.

3. Perform the Greater Banishing Ritual of the Pentagram.

4. Perform the Greater Banishing Ritual of the Hexagram, with the object of banishing all the planetary forces with the exception of Mars.

5. Take up the Holy water and circumambulate deosil saying:
"So therefore first the priest who governeth the works of fire must sprinkle with the lustral water of the loud resounding sea".

6. Take up the censer and circumambulate deosil saying:
"And when, after all the phantoms are vanished, thou shalt see that Holy formless fire, that fire which darts and flashes through the hidden depths of the Universe. Hear thou the voice of fire."

7. Circumambulate thrice deosil saying:
"Holy art thou, Lord of the Universe, Holy art thou, whom nature hath not formed, Holy art thou, the vast and mighty One, Lord of the Light and of the Darkness".

8. Perform the Greater invoking ritual of the Pentagram of Fire.

9. Say:
> *"Such a fire existeth, extending through the rushing of air. Or even a fire formless, whence cometh the image of a voice. Or even a flashing light, abounding, revolving, whirling forth and crying aloud"*

10. With the censer circumambulate deosil saluting each quarter in the sign of Leo, the kerub of fire. Say:
> *"In the sign of Leo and in the name of Michael, Great Archangel of Elemental Fire, Spirits of flame adore your Creator"*

11. Repeat the circumambulation with the censer saying.
> *"In the names and letters of the Great Southern Quadrangle, Spirits of Fire adore your Creator"*

12. Repeat the circumambulation this time saying:
> *"In the Three Great Secret Holy names of God borne upon the banners of the South, Oip Teaa Pedoce, and in the name of Edlprna the Great King of the South, Spirits of Fire adore your. Creator and be obedient unto His true and faithful servant, Amen".*

13. Facing south, vibrate very powerfully the sixth Enochian call, invoking the line *"Bitom"* from the tablet of union. Say:

> *"In the name of JHVH Tzabaoth and in the name of YHVH Aloah Va Daath yet also in the divine name Elohim, I command ye, ye dwellers in the flame, ye fiery*

> *serpents of the sign of Leo, to assist me now in this magical operation, whereby a great and mighty sword is prepared, that it be made bright with flashing flame, and do invoke ye, the Mighty Angels of the Southern Quadrangle to guide thy servitors to aid me in this Holy and Sacred task, that the sword hereby consecrated will prove an invincible ally and powerful defence, that by the power of light shed from flame it may slay and put to flight every force of evil, darkness and decay, that no phantom may stand before it and that it be thrice blessed, thrice Holy in the name of the Great Lord of Light, Amen".*

14. With the sword trace the invoking Hexagram of Mars at each of the quarters, saying *"Elohim Gibor"* while doing so.

15. Say:

> *"Thou mighty Lord of Geburah, Sphere of flame, Elohim Gibor, who art both Male and Female, King and Queen, who rideth upon an Iron Chariot with wheels of fire, I invoke thee, that by thy divine, strong and terrible Will thou may see fit to grant thy blessing upon this sword which I do offer unto thy service. Grant that with it I may defeat every power of adversity and every phantom of darkness in thy Holy and Divine Name. Grant also that I may prove a fit and proper person to hold such a terrible weapon, and I do solemnly pledge in thy Holy and Awful name that I shall never take up this weapon save in the cause of true justice and the service of Light, and do now solemnly and earnestly beseech thee to turn this blade against me should I ever break this sacred pledge. Let destruction be his who dares to stain the Holy sword of Light by darkness. This I do pledge and request of thee in the name of God Most High, Amen".*

16. Repeat the invoking hexagram of Mars in the south, saying *"Elohim Gibor"* as the hexagram is drawn.

17. Say:
> *"Thou strong and terrible archangel Khamael, I invoke thee, and beseech thee to bestow upon this Holy and Sacred sword thy powers of control and limitation of the force of fire. That it may sever only that which need severing and burn only that which needs burning. That by thy purity and strength it may perform the Divine and Holy works of fire in thy name and in the name of Elohim Gibor, Amen".*

18. Read the following invocation:
> *"There is yet a fire which flasheth, deep within the hidden depths of the Universe, a fire which flasheth amethyst radiance with a sound of iron voices rumbling in the darkness of night, whereupon a mighty Army assembles coming forth in the service of Light. And the Lord sayeth: Provide therefore of that which thou hast, that which is mine, and which thy power can extend unto in thy faculties and thy riches to show thy goodwill and ready endeavours in such things as shall be brought to pass. When thou art entered into it, whatsoever treasure there is among you, in whatever house, take it and use it, Make thee a Sword of it with two edges, that with the one thou mayest cut off Babylon's head and with the other build up Monuments and the houses of cleanliness, Godliness and understanding, that the East again may flourish, and that I may make one flock, from the Sun rising to his going down".*

19. Recite the following invocation in Enochian:
> *"Uniglag! Uniglag! ol Zacam od argedco ils Prgel Napea, Uniglag! Zodireda oi Napea"*

20. With the sword, draw invoking hexagram of Mars, vibrating *"Elohim Gibor"* while so doing.

21. With the sword, draw invoking pentagram of fire, vibrating *"Bitom"*.

22. By now the sword should have accumulated a considerable 'charge' of power and this should be apparent when tracing the above pentagrams and hexagrams. The sword may also have acquired a distinct 'personality' of its own, and the magician should skry the sword to discover any particular names and spirits associated with it. Only after such contact has been made may the next stage of the operation commence.

23. Say:

> *"In the great and splendid names of the Great Southern quadrangle I hereby summon and Invocate thee, Bziza, Banaa, Bdopa and Bpsac, thou Governing Angels of the Four Lesser angles of the Fire quadrant, by the names and powers Rzionr Nrzfm, Vadali Obava, Noalmir Oloag and Volxdo Sioda I awaken and move ever Spirit and Angel powerful in the mixture of natures to attend upon this Holy rite whereby a Mighty sword has been fashioned of iron and fire, quenched to steely hardness in the cool rushing waters and made to sing with a voice in the wind, that by thy attendance thou mayest increase its powers over any and every spirit of whatever nature, that it be rendered invincible in thy sight, and that it may prove a just and powerful government in the name of the Infinite Supreme, Lord of Light, Amen".*

Consecration of the Weapons

24. Trace the invoking pentagram of fire, saying *"Bitom"*, then say:

"In the Divine, Holy and Secret name of Aourrz, and by the power of Aloai I stir and summon ye Angels of the Fire quadrant of the Tablet of Air to note with attention this rite, and to witness the power of this Holy blade that each and every spirit of whatever element may hearken to its voice, for its voice is the voice of Fire, and of Elohim"

25. Trace invoking pentagram of fire saying *"Bitom"*. Then say:
"In the Divine, Holy and Secret name of Spmnir, and by the power of Llpiz, I stir and summon ye Angels of the Fire quadrant of the Tablet of Earth to note with attention this rite, and to witness the power of this Holy blade that each and every spirit of whatever element may hearken to its voice, for its voice is the voice of fire and of Elohim"

26. Trace the invoking pentagram of fire saying *"Bitom"*. Then say:
"In the Divine, Holy and Secret name of Iaaasd, and by the power of Atapa I stir and summon ye angels of the Fire quadrant of the Tablet of Water to note with attention this rite, and to witness the power of this Holy blade that each and every spirit of whatever element may hearken to its voice, for its voice is the voice of fire and of Elohim".

27. Pass the sword five times through the incense smoke saying:
"A sword this day is forged, on the firmament of the earth, and in the whirling, flashing fire of the Holy aethyr whereby it shall prove a severe yet just restraint upon all spirits of whatever nature, and a powerful defence against all phantoms and spirits of darkness, in thy Holy name, Elohim, so mote it be, Amen".

28. Close the temple by circumambulating thrice deosil saying:

> *"Holy art thou, Lord of the Universe, Holy art thou, whom nature hath not formed, Holy art thou, the vast and mighty One, Lord of the Light and of the Darkness".*

29. Purify the temple with water.

30. Consecrate the temple with fire.

31. Perform the Lesser Banishing Ritual of the Pentagram.

32. Perform the Greater Banishing Ritual of the Pentagram.

33. Perform the Lesser Banishing Ritual of the Hexagram.

34. Perform the Greater Banishing Ritual of the Hexagram.

35. Say:

> *"In the Holy name of Yeheshua, I now give licence to depart to all spirits summoned and imprisoned by this ceremony. Depart in peace, return to your own strange abodes with the blessing of the Most High of whom I am a true and faithful worshipper. I close this temple and draw forth the veil in the Holy name of Light supreme Amen".*

36. Make three sharp knocks.

APPENDIX I

The Lesser Banishing Rite

1. Touch the forehead saying ATEH.
2. Touch the breast and say MALKUTH.
3. Touch the right shoulder and say VE-GEBURAH.
4. Touch the left shoulder and say VE-GEDULAH.
5. Cross the hands upon breast saying LE-OLAM, AMEN.

While performing this section, which is also known as the 'Qabalistic Cross', the ritualist should visualise a beam of pure white light descending from above the head to the feet as he or she pronounces *'Ateh'* and *'Malkuth'*. As the *'Ve-Geburah'* and *'Ve-Gedulah'* sections are verbalised the light should be seen, with the inner eye, to cross the body in a limitless cross of light, light in extension. As the arms are crossed upon the breast during the final *'Le-Olam, Amen'*, part of the form of a rose-cross may be visualised. The purpose of this section of the ritual is to prepare the ritualist for the evocatory parts of the ritual which follow. It is a very important prelude to magical working and should never be omitted.

1. Face east and inscribe the Banishing Pentagram of Earth. Say: *YHVH*.

2. Walk deosil (right handed) to the south and repeat the Banishing Pentagram of Earth. Say: *ADONAI*.

3. Walk deosil to the west. Inscribe the Banishing Pentagram of Earth. Say: *EHIH*.

4. Walk deosil to the north. Inscribe the Banishing Pentagram of Earth. Say: *AGLA*.

The pentagrams are inscribed thus:

Banishing Pentagram of Earth

These should be visualised in blue-white light glowing gently with strength and purity. The god-names should be pronounced powerfully and with authority. They should be projected outwards to the very edges of the universe.

5. Extend the arms in the form of a cross and proclaim:

> "Before me Raphael, behind me Gabriel, on my right hand Michael, on my left hand Auriel, for about me shines the pentagram, and above the six-rayed star".

6. As each archangelic name is pronounced, the ritualist should construct the 'telesmatic images' of the four guardians of the quarters.

RAPHAEL is visualised as a towering being in yellow robes, his head partially hidden by clouds. He has a bow and arrows slung over his shoulder and a traveller's staff in his right hand.

MICHAEL is visualised as a towering figure in scarlet robes with Roman soldier-like bronze ornaments. He radiates power and strength. His weapon is a mighty spear.

GABRIEL is visualised as a towering figure robed in blue with silver ornaments. Over his shoulder he carries a large horn.

AURIEL is visualised as a towering figure in sombre citrine and russet robes. He may wear a large hat. He carries a large, heavily bound book from which he reads. Like Raphael, he too carries a traveller's staff.

A great deal of effort should be devoted to constructing these telesmatic images. They form the principal link between the practitioner and the rulers of the quarters. As much detail as practicable should be woven into their forms. For appropriate symbols consult the earlier sections of this book.

7. To complete the Lesser Banishing Ritual of the Pentagram, repeat the Qabalistic Cross. The entire ritual should be committed to memory before any serious magical work is undertaken.

The Greater Ritual of the Pentagram

The Greater Ritual of the Pentagram is used only after the place of working has been stabilised and prepared by the use of the Lesser Banishing Ritual. The Greater Ritual of the Pentagram is used whenever it is desired to open an elemental ritual, or it is desired to invoke the elemental rulers of a particular element. The ritual may look complex at first sight, but if you remember that to invoke a particular force you move towards that angle and to banish you move away from it, you should have few problems. The attributions of the pentagram itself are as follows:

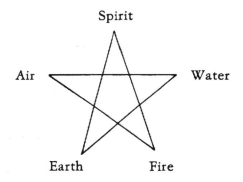

General attributions of the Pentagram

The Greater Ritual of the Pentagram also uses specific god-name attributions for each of the elements. These should also be memorised, and are as follows:

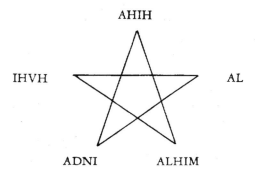

God-name attributions

From these points are derived all the patterns of invoking or banishing for each of the elemental forces. The pentagrams of Spirit are classified as Spirit Active and Spirit Passive, and for this reason there are four possible spirit pentagrams. The Active Spirit pentagrams are used with fire and air while the Passive Spirit pentagrams are used only with water and earth.

When a particular elemental force is to be invoked, as in the consecration rituals given, then use the appropriate Spirit pentagram followed by the invoking pentagram of the element required. Do not use the pentagrams of the other elements. If water is being invoked, for example, make the passive equilibrating pentagram of Spirit followed by the invoking pentagram of water at each of the four quarters. Vibrate the god-name of water *"EL"*, as each pentagram is traced. A further refinement is to visualise the kerubic sign of the element in the centre of each pentagram. This is highly effective and is a good deal easier to memorise than the traditional method of visualising the god-name in Hebrew letters. As the ritual develops over a period of time it can be expanded by

The Symbolic Weapons of Ritual Magic

the addition of various grade signs, god-form assumptions and special visualisations etc. In fact, the pentagram ritual is a cycle capable of almost infinite expansion and meaning. As such it should form a major part of the magician's regular practice.

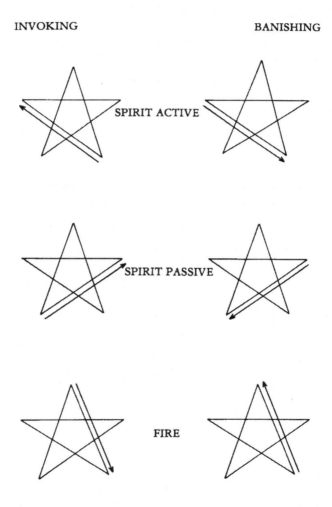

PENTAGRAMS

INVOKING		BANISHING
	WATER	
	AIR	
	EARTH	

PENTAGRAMS

The Hexagram Rituals

The hexagram is a powerful symbol representing the operation of the seven planets under the rulership of the sephiroth of the Tree of Life, and of the seven-lettered name, *Ararita*. This name is an example of a 'notariqon', a name derived from the initial letters of a phrase, in this case the Hebrew phrase *'Achad raysheethoh; achad Resh Yechidathoh; Temurathoh achod'*, which translates as 'One is His beginning; One is His individuality; His permutation is One'.

The hexagram rituals look rather complex at first sight, but if you have made the pantacle described earlier, then you have a continual reminder of the correct attribution before you upon your altar. If not, then the best way to remember the correspondences of the stations is to imagine the form of the hexagram superimposed over a diagram of the Tree of Life; in this case the top point of the hexagram is attributed to Saturn and Daath, the lowest point to Luna and Yesod; the lower left point to Mercury and Hod, the lower right point to Venus and Netzach; the upper left point to Mars and Geburah and the upper right point to Jupiter and Chesed. The sun is placed at the centre of the hexagram. In invoking the Supernals, the hexagram of Saturn is used. In the laborious Golden Dawn method the sun was invoked by tracing all six of the planetary hexagrams one after the other thus 'generating' a solar hexagram. This is needless to say, extremely time consuming and entirely unnecessary, for a solar hexagram can be generated at inner levels in its entirety then projected outwards. The same method can be used with equal success for all the other pentagrams and hexagrams the ritualist will have cause to trace during his or her work within the circle. All the arm waving tends to detract from, rather than enhance, most of the rituals I have seen. The only time physical tracing is essential is in a situation where a number of people are present, where the physical tracing helps to coordinate their visualisations. In most ritual workings, where only the practitioner or a small group of trained individuals are present, physical tracing, particularly of hexagrams, becomes a needless piece of theatrics. The inwardly generated hexagrams have proved perfectly satisfactory in the writer's opinion in every instance in which he has so far employed them. For a person with good visualisation this technique should cause few problems; but if you are a beginner, or have poor abilities at 'holding' an image for any length of time the physically traced images may prove more effective.

Another complexity of the Golden Dawn system is the altered system of attribution of the cardinal points in the hexagram rituals. Instead of the usual North-Earth, South-Fire, West-Water, East-Air system, the Golden Dawn uses North-Air, South-Earth, West-Water and East-Fire. Experimentation has shown that this complexity may be cheerfully forgotten unless particularly advanced workings are under way. Since such instances are unlikely to befall anyone requiring advice from this chapter you may safely dispense with this particular requirement.

A requirement that you should pay attention to, however, is that concerning the lunar tides when tracing the lunar hexagrams. Be careful not to work rites during the waning moon, unless they are aimed at restriction or decrease. For talismanic charging, or for consecration of a water chalice you should work with the increasing, waxing, moon.

The Lesser Ritual of the Hexagram is performed as follows:

1. Extend your arms in the form of a cross, the sign of Osiris Slain, facing east, saying: *"Yod Nun Resh Yod"*.

2. Keep your left arm extended, and raise your right arm, making the sign of the Mourning Isis. Say: *"Virgo, Isis, Mighty Mother"*.

3. Raise both arms high, making a 'V' shape, the sign of Apophis and Typhon, and say: *"Scorpio, Apophis, Destroyer"*.

4. Cross the arms upon the breast and bow the head, making the sign of Osiris Risen. Say: *"Sol, Osiris, Slain and Risen"*.

5. Gradually raise your arms, saying: *"Isis, Apophis, Osiris"*.

6. When your arms are fully raised say: *"IAO"* (pronounced Eee-Ay-Ooo).

7. Repeat the signs of the Mourning Isis, of Apophis and Typhon and of Osiris Risen saying: *"LVX, LUX, LIGHT"*

8. Fold the hands upon the breast and say: *"The Light of the Cross"*.

This completes the section sometimes known as the 'Analysis of INRI' which was mentioned earlier when discussing the magical weapons.

The Hexagram Ritual proper now begins:

1. Trace the Banishing Hexagram of Saturn whilst vibrating the name *Ararita*. Project or trace within the centre of the hexagram the figure of the planetary symbol of Saturn. Vibrate the god name YHVH ELOHIM.

2. Repeat this hexagram and names in all four quarters.

3. Repeat the Analysis of INRI to close the ritual. The hexagrams themselves are visualised or inscribed as follows. If actually tracing the patterns, then the unicursal form of hexagram developed by Aleister Crowley, and recommended by Israel Regardie, offers every advantage over the tedious and difficult traditional forms. It is this unicursal form of hexagram which I myself have found of such great benefit over the older forms, which I have discarded in favour of Crowley's system. It will be noted that Crowley's unicursal hexagrams include a pattern for the solar forces. This in itself is sufficient reason to prefer them over traditional methods.

The Symbolic Weapons of Ritual Magic

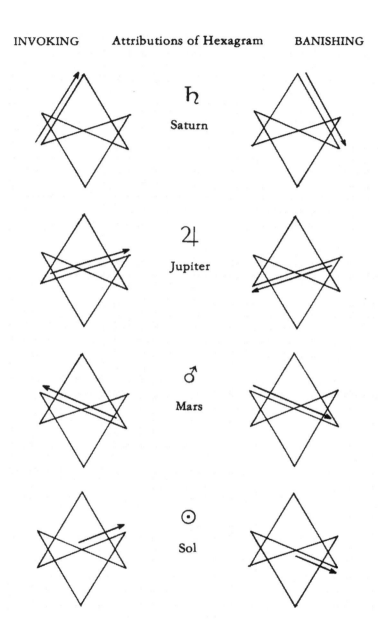

Appendices

INVOKING	Attributions of Hexagram	BANISHING

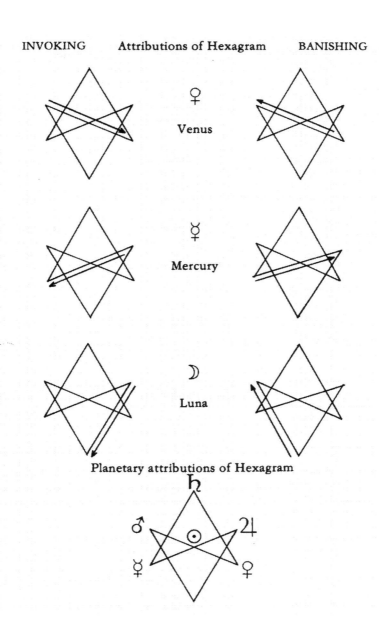

Planetary attributions of Hexagram

APPENDIX II

PREPARATION OF THE HOLY WATER

The holy water is used in all temple banishings and purifications, as well as in all rituals whenever it is desired to invoke the cleansing powers of water, for instance, in banishing undesired residual energies from the materials used in making the magical weapons. It is executed as follows.

1. Perform the Qabalistic Cross.

2. Perform the Lesser Banishing Ritual of the Pentagram.

3. Place some salt in a small earthenware dish upon the altar. Extend your hand over it saying:

> *"Creature of Earth, I conjure Thee, that there be banished from whatever place thou art used every power of adversity and evil, every force of deceit and every phantom of darkness. In the Holy names and powers of Earth, be thou Holy, Amen".*

During this part of the operation you should strongly visualise the cleansing and preserving powers of salt, infused with Holy Light.

4. Place before you some pure water in a glass or chalice. Spring water or rainwater is best; water from a sacred site or holy well is best of all. Extend your hand over it saying:

> *"Creature of water, I conjure thee, that there be cleansed from whatever place thou art used every power of adversity and evil, every force of deceit and every phantom of darkness. In the Holy names and powers of water, be thou Holy, Amen"*

You should visualise the flowing and cleansing powers of water manifested within the glass or chalice, infused with the Holy Light while performing this operation.

5. Cast a little of the consecrated salt into the water, saying:
> *"Sign of Ox and Eagle conjoined, Powers of Earth and Water made one, Wings of Spirit exalting Form, In the Holy names and powers of Light be pure".*

The holy water is now prepared and may be employed in any ritual situation where its use is demanded.

APPENDIX III

PRONUNCIATION OF ENOCHIAN

The pronunciation given here is that used by the Order of the Golden Dawn and is not intended as a definitive statement of original Enochian speech. The indications are that the Enochian received by Dee and Kelley was pronounced entirely differently from the method employed in the Golden Dawn. However, it is the Golden Dawn system which has proved of consistent worth in magical ritual and for this reason is to be recommended to the student.

A: *AH*	L: *EL*	V: *VEE*
B: *BA*	M: *EM*	X: *ECKS*
C: *K*	N: *EN*	Y: *YE*
D: *DEE*	O: *OH*	Z: *ZODE*
E: *EE*	P: *PEE*	
F: *EF*	Q: *KWA*	
G: *GLA*	R: *RA*	
H: *HA*	S: *ESS*	
I: *E*	T: *TAY*	
K: *KAY*	U: *OO*	

Certain letters, such as UN, appear interchangeable in early manuscripts and it is far from clear if this is intentional or due to an error.

As a general rule each letter of the Enochian language is pronounced separately, except where the presence of vowels permits lengthier vocalisation.

Appendices

It is really a question of getting used to the peculiar rhythm and accent. For this reason a few examples, with phonetic pronunciation, are given below:

BATAIVAH = Bat-Ah-ee-Vah
AOZM = Ay-Oh-Zode-Pi
EMPEH = Em-Peh
ICZHICIAL = Ik-Zode-Hitch-Ial
AHMLICV = Ah-Em-el-e-k-Vee
SONIZNT = Son-e-Zodent
HIPOTGA = Hip-oh-tay-Gah
EXARP = Ecks-ar-Pay

APPENDIX IV

The Hebrew Names used upon the Weapons

These names and letters are provided full size for making templates from for use in inlaying. Draw or photocopy this page to obtain working outlines.

THE CHALICE

אל　　גבריאל

EL　　　GABRIEL

THE WAND

יהוה　　רפאל

YHVH　　RAPHAEL

THE DAGGER

אלהים　　מיכאל

ELOHIM　　MICHAEL

THE PANTACLE

אוריאל   אדני

ADONAI　　　AURIEL

THE SWORD

גבור   אלהים

ELOHIM　　　GIBOR

כמאל

KHAMAEL

The Symbolic Weapons of Ritual Magic

TABLE 1: THE SEPHIROTH

TITLE	GOD-NAME	ARCHANGEL	ANGEL ORDER	MUNDANE CHAKRA	OTHER TITLE
KETHER	EHEIEH	METATRON	CHAIOTH ha QADESH	PRIMUM MOBILE	THE CROWN
CHOCKMAH	YHVH	RATZIEL	AUPHANIM	THE ZODIAC	WISDOM
BINAH	IHVH ELOHIM	TZAPHKIEL	ARALIM	SATURN	UNDERSTANDING
CHESED	EL	TZADKIEL	CHASMALIM	JUPITER	MERCY
GEBURAH	ELOHIM GIBOR	KHAMAEL	SERAPHIM	MARS	SEVERITY
TIPHARETH	YHVH ALOAH va DAAT	MICHAEL*	MALAKIM	SOL	BEAUTY
NETZACH	JHVH TZABAOTH	HANIEL	ELOHIM	VENUS	VICTORY
HOD	ELOHIM TZABAOTH	RAPHAEL*	BENI ELOHIM	MERCURY	GLORY
YESOD	SHADDAI el CHAI	GABRIEL*	AISHIM	LUNA	FOUNDATION
MALKUTH	ADONAI MALAKH	SANDALPHON*	KERUBIM	EARTH	KINGDOM

* *The Elements:*
MICHAEL *is attributed to Fire.*
RAPHAEL *is attributed to Air.*
GABRIEL *is attributed to Water.*
AURIEL *is attributed to Earth.*

* *The Elements:*
MICHAEL *is attributed to Fire.*
RAPHAEL *is attributed to Water.*
GABRIEL *is attributed to Water.*
AURIEL *is attributed to Earth.*
The Archangel Auriel is a variant form of Sandalphon and also appears under a different guise as Haniel the Archangel of Netzach. Auriel is concerned with 'earth to earth' aspects whilst Sandalphon is a rather special Archangel who is linked closely with Metatron the Archangel of Kether.

Appendices

TABLE 2: THE COLOUR SCALES

TITLE	KING SCALE	QUEEN SCALE	EMPEROR SCALE	EMPRESS SCALE
KETHER	BRILLIANCE	WHITE BRILLIANCE	WHITE BRILLIANCE	WHITE-FLECKED GOLD
CHOCKMAH	SOFT BLUE	GREY	BLUE PEARL	WHITE-FLECKED RED, BLUE AND YELLOW
BINAH	CRIMSON	BLACK	DARK BROWN	GREY-FLECKED PINK
CHESED	DARK VIOLET	BLUE	DEEP PURPLE	DEEP AZURE-FLECKED YELLOW
GEBURAH	ORANGE	SCARLET	BRIGHT SCARLET	RED-FLECKED BLACK
TIPHARETH	CLEAR ROSE PINK	GOLD YELLOW	RICH SALMON	GOLD AMBER
NETZACH	AMBER	EMERALD GREEN	YELLOW GREEN	OLIVE-FLECKED GOLD
HOD	VIOLET PURPLE	BRIGHT ORANGE	RED-RUSSET	YELLOW-BROWN-FLECKED WHITE
YESOD	INDIGO	VIOLET	DARK PURPLE	CITRINE-FLECKED AZURE
MALKUTH	YELLOW	CITRINE, OLIVE, BLACK AND RUSSET	AS BEFORE, FLECKED GOLD	BLACK-RAYED YELLOW

KING SCALE – Archetypal world of Atziluth.
QUEEN SCALE – Archangelic creative world of Briah.
EMPEROR SCALE – Angelic formative world of Yetzirah.
EMPRESS SCALE – Elemental, planetary and expressive world of Assiah.

TABLE 3: RITUAL CORRESPONDENCES OF WOODS, METALS, PRECIOUS STONES, etc.

TITLE	WOODS	METALS	PRECIOUS STONES	BASIC INCENSE
KETHER:	ALMOND	NONE APPLY	DIAMOND	AMBERGRIS ESSENCE
CHOCKMAH:	AMARANTH, HOLLY	ELECTRUM MAGICUM	RUBY	MUSK ESSENCE
BINAH:	CYPRESS, YEW, ELM	LEAD	SAPPHIRE	CIVET, MYRRH, SCAMMONY
CHESED:	OLIVE, CEDAR, BOX	TIN, BRASS	LAPIS LAZULI	COPAL, ALOESWOOD, SAFFRON
GEBURAH:	OAK, PADAUK, EBONY	IRON, BRASS, BRONZE	AMETHYST	OPOPONAX, DRAGONS BLOOD
TIPHARETH:	ASH, WALNUT, ACACIA	GOLD, BRASS	TOPAZ	FRANKINCENSE, MYRRH, CINNAMON
NETZACH:	APPLE, LAUREL, ROSEWOOD	COPPER, BRASS	EMERALD	BENZOIN, ROSE, CIVET
HOD:	SATINWOOD, HAZELWOOD	ALUMINIUM	OPAL	MACE, MASTIC, SANDALWOOD
YESOD:	WILLOW, SYCAMORE	SILVER	QUARTZ, PEARL, CRYSTAL	CAMPHOR, CUCUMBER SEEDS
MALKUTH:	ASH, WILLOW, OAK	MAGNETIC IRON	JET, AMBER, OBSIDION	STORAX, RED SANDAL, DITTANY

Note:
Common sense is frequently a better guide than tradition where correspondences are concerned. Hence, aluminium is suggested in place of quicksilver and brass suggested as a viable alternative to gold. Where the precious stones are concerned, imitations are every bit as effective as the genuine article. With perfumes it is best to avoid animal derived substances like civet, musk or ambergris and instead use one of the excellent synthetics now available.

BIBLIOGRAPHY

The editions listed are those I have used myself or found most readily available. Other editions are frequently also available.

CASAUBON, MERIC
Of Spirits and Apparitions (1659). Reprinted 1974
CROWLEY, ALEISTER
Magick (Routledge and Kegan Paul, 1973).
777 and other Qabalistic Writings (Weiser, 1977).
FORTUNE, DION
The Mystical Qabalah (Benn, 1935).
FRAZER J. G.
The Golden Bough (Macmillan, 1957).
GRAVES, ROBERT
The White Goddess (Faber, 1961).
GRAVES, TOM
Needles of Stone (Turnstone Press, 1978).
GRAY, W. G.
The Ladder of Lights (Helios Book Service, 1968).
Magical Ritual Methods (Weiser, 1980).
KNIGHT, GARETH
A Practical Guide to Qabalistic Symbolism, Vols. 1 and 2 (Helios Book Service, 1976).
LAYCOCK, DONALD
The Complete Enochian Dictionary (Askin, 1978).
LEVI, ELIPHAS
Transcendental Magic (Rider, 1972).

MATHERS, S. L.
The Key of Solomon the King (Routledge and Kegan Paul, 1972).
The Sacred Magic of Abramelin the Mage (Thorsons, 1976).
The Kabbalah Unveiled
REGARDIE, ISRAEL
The Golden Dawn (Llewellyn Publications, 1971).
The Philosopher's Stone (Llewellyn Publications, 1974).
Ceremonial Magic (Aquarian Press, 1980).
The Tree of Life (Rider, 1932).
Foundations of Practical Magic (Aquarian Press, 1979).
VINCI, LEO
Gmicalzoma! (Regency Press, 1976).
WESTCOTT, W.
The Sepher Yetzirah (Weiser, 1980).

INDEX

Abramelin the Mage, 88, 97

Adonai Malakh, 71

Adonis, 23

Aima, 20,21,24

Air, element of 7,8,10, 25,26, 31-35, 37, 38, 51, 74, 76, 79, 90, 96, 102, 130, 165

Aishim, 48, 55-56, 71

Akasha, 48, 68

Aleph, 20, 21, 79

Altar, 86

Aima, 20-21, 24

Ana, 12

Anat, 19

Angels, 9, 49, 73,

Anointing, 87-88

Aphrodite, 21, 23, 35

Apron, 34-35, 74, 87

Aquarius, 9, 27,70, 90, 126

Aralim, the, 22

Archangels, 9,10, 32, 75

Ark, symbolism of, 11, 30

Arrow, symbolism of, 26-29, 68

Arthur, King, 11, 41, 62

Assiah, 9, 36

Astral light, 48

Astral plane, 56

Athame, 11

Atlas, 72

Atziluth, world of 9, 36,

Index

Auphanim, 42
Auriel, 37, 68-69, 90, 153

'Beast 666', 14-15
Beni-Elohim, 38-39
Binah, 19-24, 41-42, 49, 62-66, 80, 82, 88-89
Blood, 4, 7, 14-18, 20, 50-51
Briah, world of, 9, 36

Caduceus, 34, 97
Cauldron, symbol, 10-12, 19, 24
Celestial Images, Book of, (Highfield) 3, 76
Censer, 84-85
Chalice (Cup) 4-24, 49, 50, 62; constructing, 92-96; consecrating, 117-123
Chasmalim, 39
Chioth ha Kadosh, 70
Chesed, 18, 31, 33, 36, 37-41, 78-80, 86, 158
Chokmah, 20, 21, 22, 37, 41-43, 63, 79, 80-82, 86, 88, 89
Christ, 18, 54, 55, 77, 85
Corn King, 18
Crowley, Aleister, 14-15, 31-32, 59, 75, 83, 161
Cup, see Chalice
'Cup of Babalon', 14
Cybele, 23
Daath, 18, 49, 53, 158
Dee, Dr. John, 115, 166
Demeter, 23
Diana, 12, 30, 72
Disc, see Pantacle
Divine King, 11, 16-17, 19, 29, 50, 51, 56, 76
Drawing down the Moon, 12

Index

Eagle (Kerubim), 9, 70, 93, 120
Earth, element of, 7, 8, 67-68, 75, 90
Earth, archangel of, 69
Elemental lamps, 90
Elemental spirits, 8
Elohim Gibor, 60, 103,
Elohim Sabaoth, 33, 52, 73
Emerald Tablet, 11
Empress colours, 36
Enochian, 115-116, 166-167
Evil, 23, 37, 56-57, 62, 77
Evocation, 65, 69, 75

Feminine principle, 12, 42
Fertility, 7, 10, 13, 17, 21, 48
Fire, element of, 7, 8, 11, 13-14, 45-47, 59
Fire dagger, 46, 60, 68, 107-110, 130-136
Fortune, Dion 48, 71
Frazer, Sir J. G., 10
Freemasonry, 35

Gabriel, 10, 11, 15, 48-49, 68, 71, 153
Geburah, 14, 18, 19-20, 38-39, 45, 51, 54, 56-62, 86, 146
Geburic fire, 13
Gemini, 27
Girdle, 87
'Gluten of the White Eagle', 14
Goetia of Solomon the King, (tr. Mathers) 83,
Golden Dawn, Hermetic Order of, 77, 88, 93, 97, 115, 158-159
Graves, Robert, 10
Great Mother, 20, 41
Great Rite, the 11,

Index

Great Work, the, 17, 55, 70, 82, 86, 89

Hag, aspect (of moon), 12, 21
Haniel, 15
Hebrew names, 100, 168
Hecate, 12
Hell, 63, 65,
Hermes, 30, 35
Hexagram rituals, 158-163
Hod, 15, 28, 30-35, 41, 63, 73-76, 87
Holy Blood, 4, 16-17, 50
Holy Ghost, 14, 48-49, 55, 65, 72
Holy Grail, 16-17, 50
Holy Names, 75
Holy Oil, 87-88, 97, 117
Holy Water, preparation, 164-165
Homosexual magic, 15, 32
Horn, symbolism of, 10-11, 40, 49, 68,
Horus, Eye of, 23, 62

IHVH, Elohim, 23
Initiation, 15, 16, 30-31, 52, 87
Inner Robe of Glory, 88-89
Ishtar, 65
Isis, 23, 77, 160

Kali, 19
Karma, 40
Kelley, Edward, 115, 166
Kerubim, 9, 48, 70
Kether, 6, 36, 53, 55-56, 68, 71
Khamael, 23, 37, 39, 59, 60-62, 103

Index

Kingship, 40-41
Klipothic, 57, 76

Lamed, 79
Lamen, 86
Lamp, 15-16, 52, 86-87, 90
Lance (Spear), 11, 13-14, 19, 74
Leo, 9, 14, 70, 90, 133
Levi, Eliphas, 31,
Liber 777 (Crowley), 75, 83,
Lion (Kerubim), 9, 14, 70
Love, 37-38, 50
Lucifer, 17, 24, 62
Lunar, symbolism of, 4, 12, 14, 22, 71-73

Magic, nature of, 2, 13, 24, 73, 91
Malkuth, 6-10, 26-29, 46-49, 68-71
Man (Kerubim), 9, 70
Mars, 14, 16, 19-20, 51, 57-58, 60
Mathers, S. L., 31, 88
Mercury, 31, 53, 158
Metatron, 70-71
Michael, 18, 36-37, 47, 54, 60, 68, 109
Moon, 11-12, 21-22, 30, 56, 65, 71-72, 91
Mother aspect (of moon) 21
Mundane chakras, 11, 18, 22, 31, 39, 41, 42,
Mystical Qabalah, the (Dion Fortune), 48

Netzach, 13-17, 50-52, 86, 87
Nine, symbolism of, 22

Orpheus, 51

Osiris, 18, 23, 54-55, 85
Outer Robe of Concealment, 88
Ox (Kerubim), 9, 21, 70, 79

Pantacle (Disc), 59, 67-83, 111-114, 137-143
Passion, 13, 87
Pentagram rituals, 151-157
Phallic (symbolism), 14, 25, 29, 41-43
Pillars (temple), 89-90

Qabalah, definition, 66

Raphael, 18, 28, 32-33, 37, 68
Ratziel, 42, 82-83
Rebirth, 11
Regardie, Israel, 97, 161
Regeneration, 11, 40
Ring, 86
Rod (Wand), 25-44, 96-101, 124-130

Sacrifice, symbolism of, 18-19, 29, 40, 50-51, 56, 76
Salamanders (elementals), 47
Samael, 37
Sandalphon, 70-71
Sandals, symbolism of, 34, 87
Satan, 23, 48, 62
Saturn (Kronos), 22-23
'Scarlet Woman', 14, 24, 52,
Schemhamphoresch, 73, 82
Scorpio, 9, 14, 70, 77, 90
Sepher Yetzirah, 63, 78,
Seraphim, 59-60, 65

Index

Sex energies, 13, 45
Sexual magic, 14-15, 17, 30, 49
Shadai el Chai, 11
Shield, 35, 59, 68
Solar Logos, 14, 18, 36
Standing Stones (megaliths), 29, 45
Sword, 27, 28, 45-66, 102-106, 144-150
Sylphs (elementals), 28
Symbolism, 5-6, 22, 25, 74, 79

Tarot, 30
Taurus, 9, 52, 70, 90
Telesmatic Images, 75-76, 153
Tetragrammaton, 42
Thoth, 30, 49, 72
Thrones, see Aralim
Tiphareth, 17-19, 35-37, 47, 52-56, 60, 76-78
Tzadkiel, 39
Tzaphkiel, 22-23, 62

Undines (elementals), 8

Vagina, symbolism of, 10, 30
Venus, 12, 16, 17, 21, 24, 31, 50-52, 65, 87
Virgin, aspect (of moon), 12, 21
Virgin Mary (Stella Maris), 23, 64

Wand, see Rod
Water, 7-8, 10-11, 13, 15, 49, 71, 74, 92
Water, Holy, preparation of, 164-165
Wells, H. G., 38

Western Mystery Tradition, 2, 3
White Goddess, The, (Graves), 10
Wicca, 11, 36

Yahwe, 23
Yesod, 10-13, 14, 30, 48-49, 55, 71-73, 75, 87
Yetzirah, world of, 9, 36
Yhvh Aloah va Daath, 24, 82
Yod, (Hebrew letter) 21, 77, 159

Zodiac, 9, 41, 42, 70, 82, 137

For the latest information on forthcoming titles or to contact our authors, please visit:

www.pyramidionpress.com